Tired of arguing with your Kids?

Curran's timely book presents practical ideas in a critical area of family life. Her many anecdotal examples are easily read and convey the comforting awareness that all families face these trials, the reader is not alone.

George Doub, M.Div.
Family Wellness Association
San Jose, CA

A great book! Curran provides the help we need with the nitty gritty of what to actually do and say. It's one thing for an author to tell us to set boundaries or ignore fights and whining, it's quite another to tell us how to get "unhooked."

Joan Comeau, Ph.D.
Family Information Services
Minneapolis, MN

A book full of lots and lots of wonderful responses to help parents deal with children's creative and challenging behaviors— all presented with a sense of humor and insight.

Marge Peterson
Child Development Center
Denver, CO

Practical, insightful, easy to read and put in practice—there are so many ways this is a great book.

Jim and Kathy McGinnis
The Institute for Peace and Justice
St. Louis, MO

Uncomplicated solutions to real day-to-day family issues. Curran's best yet!

Linda Johnston
Practical Parent Education
Dallas, TX

dolores curran

Tired of arguing with your Kids?

wisdom from parents
who have been there

SORIN BOOKS   Notre Dame, IN

Acknowledgments

I am grateful for the contributions of the following colleagues who read my early manuscript with a caring but perceptive and objective eye. This is a much better book than it would have been without their insights and suggestions.

Joan Comeau, Ph.D., *Founder and Director, Family Information Services, Minneapolis, MN*

George Doub, M.Div., *Founder and Director, Family Wellness Association, San Jose, CA*

Linda Johnston, Ph.D. Cand., *Executive Director, Practical Parent Education, Dallas, TX*

Jim McGinnis, Ph.D., and Kathy McGinnis, M.A., *Co-founders and Directors, The Institute for Peace and Justice, St. Louis, MO*

Marge Petersen, M.A., *Director, Child Development Center, Metropolitan State College, Denver, CO*

Library of Congress Catalog Card Number: 99-61901

ISBN: 1-893732-06-1

Cover design: K.H. Coney

Interior text design: Brian C. Conley

Dedication

I dedicate this book to the parents and parent-educators who shared your stories, wisdom and humor with me and the readers. You are our sages. Thank you for your willingness to pass along what you have learned, especially the message parents yearn to learn: "Lighten up and enjoy the trip."

CONTENTS

INTRODUCTION

"That's not fair," my young son whined in a familiar tone of righteousness.

I was bone weary, the way young mothers get at about five p.m., so I responded dispiritedly, "You're probably right."

He stopped, confused. Why wasn't I rising to his bait—defending, arguing, explaining—as I usually did when his life needed a bit of spice? He eyed me warily and then asked, "What's wrong, Mom?"

"I'm too tired to argue."

"Oh, okay." And he went off to perform whatever chore I had assigned him, most likely the onerous task of picking up his socks or soldiers.

It was a revelation to me, this idea that I could refuse to argue with him without losing authority. Naively, I thought I had uncovered the key to hassle-free parenting. When he invoked his classic parent-baiting charge, "That's not fair," all I had to say was, "You're probably right," and that would end all arguments.

I was wrong, of course. Kids are both creative and resilient when it comes to training parents. The next time I used the technique, my son put his hands on his hips and said defiantly, "Well, if it's not fair, then I shouldn't have to do it."

Familiar bile rose in me but I resisted the urge to turn this into the 900th replay of his favorite leisure time activity—arguing with Mom. I sighed, "I know how you feel. Doesn't it drive you crazy to have to do things that aren't fair?"

This stopped him for a second or two and then he said uncertainly, "Well, I'm not going to do it." I smiled at him. He shifted and said, "You can't make me." I smiled again and as he turned to walk away I said, "When you finish, let me know," and this time *I* walked away.

That worked a few times and then he decided to call my bluff, refusing to carry out my wishes. Flushed with earlier victories, I wasn't ready to concede easily. I simply waited until it was time for his snack or TV or outside play or dinner or whatever it was he enjoyed doing, and then I said, "No chores, no fun."

He got the idea. When he discovered I really meant I wasn't going to argue but was going to stick with previously stated consequences, his behavior changed. "It isn't fair," didn't work any longer. It's hard to argue with someone who agrees with you.

That scenario took place many years and three children ago but I remain convinced that 80% or more of the arguments we have with children are non-arguments. Worse, they are draining and unproductive. If parents possess, say, one hundred units of daily energy to deal with children and we expend them on non-issues which deserve non-answers, it's little wonder that we are exhausted, impatient, and disenchanted with children so much of the time.

I am also convinced that parents recognize the futility of most arguments with children but they don't know the right words to invoke to initiate change. That's what this book is all about. In the past several years, I have collected parents' effective responses to children's classic questions, complaints, charges, and arguments. I wish I could write that these are my own wise and original responses but most of them come from parents who have decided that family life isn't worth the ongoing argumentation that passes as communication in many American families.

We parents need to share our experiences and wisdom. I wish I had some of these creative responses twenty years ago when I was arguing with a five-year-old whether meatloaf was good or yucky. Back then, I argued. Today, I'd simply agree, smile, and serve it. Older parents, parents whose children had grown up and left home, were my primary resources. They had learned to keep conflict in perspective. They had discovered that parents can ignore arguments without losing respect or control. And they were willing to share both their techniques and failures, bless them.

In one of my parenting seminars, a young mother voiced a familiar frustration. "We seem to hassle over the same things day after day. How clean is clean, as in a room? How long is a minute, as in 'just a minute'? How do I get one to stop *looking* at another? I get so tired of these arguments, but they never end." Other parents nodded in agreement with her words.

A grandmother, who was attending along with her son and daughter-in-law, was elbowed by her son who said in a loud stage whisper, "Tell them how you handled it, Mom."

They both laughed and she shared her solution. "I felt the same way you do and one day I just had had enough, so I told the kids that from then on, arguments about cleaning their rooms would be referred to as Argument A. The one about who sits on the hump in the backseat was Argument B and so on. I said it would save us words and energy if we just said, 'Argument M' instead of repeating the same words every time there was a hassle. It became kind of a game and it worked for us."

Oh, how I wish I had thought of that when my three were young and had colossal staying power in discussions over who performed which chore the last time. I remained the patient panel discussion leader for just so long and then exploded, not recognizing that the issue wasn't as important to them as the argument. If I were reparenting these same three today, I would agree, ignore, and smile more—and defend, explain, and mediate less.

I would not play, as I once did, the presiding judge when they fought during play, asking patiently, "Now, who started this? Then what happened? Who had the ball first? Why did you grab it? Did you say that to him? You know that's not permitted in this family."

Eventually, as I matured in age and parenting, I learned to allow their conflicts to be *their* conflicts, recognizing their need to learn to get along without a parent referee. I simply asked them to go out of range of my hearing if they wanted to fight. If the level of conflict became too heated, I said, "If you can't play together, you can't play together," and separated them for awhile explaining, "Maybe you'll be able to get along better in an hour because you'll be older then."

Like many young parents, I thought I was alone in rehashing kids' classic charges, countercharges, complaints, comments and questions. I thought good parents didn't have to deal with these frustrating drains of energy and that if I found the magic key, my children wouldn't argue with me. Rather, they would smile and acquiesce to my wishes and authority.

Wrong. Children argue. It's as simple as that. *Good* children argue with good parents. One might even suggest that arguing is part of a child's job description, a socializing responsibility in today's Western family culture. Submissive acquiescence is perceived as weakness rather than virtue in modern children. Gone are the days where good children were seen and not heard. Few of us want those days back.

But when conventional wisdom suggested that we needed to listen and talk with children rather than silence them, we swung wildly to the other extreme, believing that we need to listen to and negotiate every issue every time our children challenge us. So, today, even simple requests become court cases and parents become weary to the point of enduring their children instead of enjoying them.

Children don't deliberately set out to frustrate us. They do test us, however, because they have little power. Powerless people often resort to manipulation as the only way to get their way so children often manipulate parents in the form of ongoing argumentation, whines, endless "whys," and annoying non-verbal behaviors.

When parents realize they are being manipulated, they are more confident in responding than when they feel they are being challenged. So, when the frustration level begins to elevate, wise parents ask themselves first, "Is this a genuine issue or am I being manipulated and am I rising to the bait?"

For the past twenty years, I have taught parenting classes and conducted seminars for thousands of parents. I hear the same complaints over and over. I've discovered that when I or someone else in the group offers a quick response to children's classic arguments, parents are delighted. "I'm going to try that," they exclaim, jotting down the idea or response.

Several times when a number of parents shared their wisdom and responses, other parents asked, "Are these collected anywhere? They're wonderful, but I'll never remember them." So here they are. I have taken the most familiar argument starters and given several responses to each. Parenting styles differ, so I have tried to offer a variety of responses to fit a diversity of parents.

To some parents these responses may seem flippant, even unkind. If so, they shouldn't use them. Parents who use responses that do not fit their personalities and parenting styles will find themselves uncomfortable in invoking those responses.

Much depends on how a specific response is delivered. I'll cite a personal example. My mother, who bore and reared seven children in a pace of ten years, developed a non-answer to our non-arguments. When she tired of answering our silly questions or repeated whys, she would say brightly, "strawberry shortcake." It was her way of letting us know that she wasn't going to get hooked into further argument. When we heard "strawberry shortcake," we knew it was futile to continue our tirade.

If, however, we persisted and whined, "What do you mean, 'strawberry shortcake'? What's that got to do with it?" she smiled and replied, "cornbread," or "maple syrup." Eventually we tired of the game and went off miffed, forgetting the issue within a matter of minutes.

Many parents feel terrible if their children go off miffed or unhappy. These parents can't live with unpopularity and come to question their own competence in dealing with children, believing that children should always be happy and satisfied even if parents are stressed beyond their limits. These parents live with guilt and die a little inside when their child says, "I don't like you, " or "I hate you," or "I wish you weren't my dad."

Readers will find several rules in this book. One is that it's okay to be unpopular at times. Occasional unpopularity, in fact, goes with the territory. When a child hooks a parent's guilt by saying, "You're a mean mother," the parent has several options—anger, guilt, apology, or agreement. I prefer agreement because anger drains energy, and apology and guilt, unless justified, signify defeat. "Yes, I suppose you're right," to such a charge tells the child that the parent is not going to get hooked into a conflict.

A cardinal caution here. I am not suggesting that parents should always cut off children's arguments. There are times when we are *unfair*, times that we need to listen, times when we need to explain our actions. These are the times we need to stop what we're doing and listen and respond with care.

Our task is to learn to weed out the important arguments from the non-arguments. When we are able to do this, we can spend those precious units of energy on the really important feelings and issues of children. Non-arguments are those which are initiated by children to get parental attention, to alleviate boredom, to resist responsibility, and to contest parental authority. Non-arguments are those that are never settled and put away but rather are replayed daily as part of the family ritual. This book is devoted to dealing with these frustrating replays so we can preserve our energy to deal with issues which deserve our attention.

CHAPTER ONE

Detach, Detach, Detach

Beth Hanks looked at the clock. "Marcy, it's time to get dressed for your piano lesson."

Marcy, reluctant to abandon her after-school television, argued, "I look okay. Why do I have to change?"

"Play clothes are for play. Put on something nicer out of respect for Mrs. Cronin."

Marcy persisted, "But I wore these last time."

Beth smiled and replied firmly but without emotion, "Call me when you're ready, and I'll be happy to give you a ride."

Beth's handling of a potential argument deserves a top grade. She didn't order Marcy to change her clothes but informed her that it was time to change. When Marcy demanded a reason, Beth supplied two. When Marcy attempted to engage her in further non-essential argument, Beth refused to get hooked. Finally, Beth subtly mentioned a consequence: "I'll drive you," the inference being, "If you don't change, you can get there on your own." Withdrawal of service is one of the most effective and under-utilized consequences available to parents.

Parents are not required to argue. Detaching or refusing to get hooked into meaningless argument with children is the fundamental key to minimizing family hassles. Children get very adept at hooking parents into arguments. They know which buttons to push, which issues and questions are likely to engage their parents' emotions. These vary from parent to parent. What hooks one may not phase another.

I, for example, didn't feel annoyed when I heard, "What's for dinner?" but dozens of other mothers have indicated that this one drives them up the wall because they are then expected to support what they prepare before it is even tasted. As one weary mother said, "It's hard enough to cook dinner but to have to defend it is outrageous."

When my children asked what was for dinner, I simply replied, "I don't know." Often I wasn't sure, but even if I did know, the specter of having no dinner is more frightening to a child than goulash. I detached from potential whining by showing disinterest. Sometimes, I replied, "A big surprise." Or, "Two choices: Take it or Leave it." I wish I had come up with a response I heard from a mother recently, "Gee, I don't know, but it's brown and wet and sort of lumpy. What do you think we should call it?"

These responses are all detaching devices. How do parents learn to detach? The most important skill to work on is **tone of voice**. It's the cue children listen for when they initiate non-arguments. If a parent responds evenly in a non-emotional tone, children instinctively sense that the parent isn't going to get hooked into meaningless argument.

If, on the other hand, parents react defensively or with anger, children know they have hooked them. It's essential that parents recognize the simple truth that it takes two to argue. Children are almost required to argue but parents possess the choice of refusal. We don't have to get hooked. We are the ones who choose to detach or be hooked.

For parents who find it difficult to establish an even tone of voice in responding to children's arguments, here are a few suggestions.

Respond as if one were discussing an issue with a four-year-old who, say, argues that the sun is the moon. Parents don't waste a lot of emotion on giving reasons to toddlers because toddlers cannot reason. Parents smile and agree because they recognize the futility of arguing the issue. So, imagining that the argumentative child standing in front of us is three or four, regardless of his or her true age, and responding in the same fashion and tone of voice may be helpful for the parent trying to learn detachment skills.

A second technique calls for adopting the tone we use when we are bone tired. At the end of a long day, when the parent is weary of dealing with questions, but a child tries to engage in a non-essential issue, the parent often reacts unemotionally. The energy to argue is gone, used up during the course of the day. If parents who are striving to develop new detaching skills learn to call up this same tone of voice during the day, they will find it easier in establishing an effective tone of detachment.

Finally, parents can regard non-arguments with children in much the same way they regard someone who has had too much to drink and wants to argue. When caught in this situation, most of us just smile and agree. Again, we recognize the foolishness of attempting to reason with someone who doesn't want to reason but just wants to argue—an apt description of the child trying to hook parents into endless and meaningless debate.

Sarcasm heats up most arguments. Sarcasm is a communication killer and parents who have gotten into the habit of using it need to recognize its cost. It usually escalates rather than defuses conflict; it can initiate immense anger; and, most costly, it becomes a family habit. Parents who routinely use sarcasm with children are often dismayed to hear their children use it unkindly with one another.

All families have a mood. In some, it's positive and others negative. Sarcasm generally leads to a negative mood or atmosphere. In families where quick, nasty rejoinders pass for communication, the general mood becomes unpleasant, even ugly.

In my earlier books, I note that sarcasm is frequently transferred by parents from the workplace to homeplace. Parents become so accustomed to responding in a clever put-down style at work that they don't even realize they are doing it with those they love. Children become victims because they can't respond in kind. Such parents often call their sarcasm humor but there's very little funny about it.

Once, in a parenting workshop, a sarcastic father named "a sense of play and humor" as their family's top strength. His fifteen-year-old son, however, placed it fourteenth in a list of fifteen. The dad was amazed and said to his son, "I thought we were pretty funny."

"You are, Dad, but it kills," the son replied. And he's right. Sarcasm kills conversation and communication because it's unanswerable. Many of the parent responses offered in this book lend themselves to sarcasm so parents must be very cautious of tone while using them. The words are less important than the tone of voice chosen. Even "I'm sorry" or "thank you" can be intoned sarcastically, so the handiness of these responses depends on the tone the parent chooses.

Parents can respond to their children using a number of different tones: thoughtful, quizzical, apologetic, commanding, empathetic, angry, and incredulous are just a few of many. Let's look at an example of how a parent might respond to a child's complaint in a variety of tones.

Six-year-old Mark is running late this morning. "I can't find my shoes," he wails. His parent can respond in any of the following ways:

Commanding: "Find them right now. You're already late."

Aggrieved: "I've told you a thousand times to put your shoes in the same place when you go to bed. Then you'd know where they are. Now I have to stop feeding the baby to help you find them. You don't think about anybody but yourself, do you?"

Angry: "Again? Well, young man, you're just going to have to be late because I'm not looking for them. And if the teacher gets mad at you, that's fine with me."

Sarcastic: "I can't imagine why you can't find your shoes when you always put them where they belong."

Quizzical: "Really? Those shoes get around, don't they? I'm sure you'll find them somewhere. You always do."

Lighthearted: "What a bummer. We need to train our dog to sniff out shoes in this family, don't we?"

Empathetic: "That's too bad, honey. I hate it when I have to search for my shoes."

The first four of these responses indicate that the parent's emotions have been aroused and precious emotional energy has been drained. The last three are non-emotional and clearly imply that finding the child's shoes is **his** chore. Which is likely to be more effective? And which has the least emotional cost to the parent?

While tone of voice is fundamental to detaching, **a second detaching skill involves facial expression and body language.** Children who are trying to hook us watch our expressions closely. Often they position themselves to observe parent reaction before initiating a complaint. One of my sons had the habit of walking up to me, facing himself squarely in front of me, and peering up into my face before he asked for something he already knew he couldn't have or do.

One method of forestalling non-arguments with children is simply smiling indulgently to ourselves as we do when children say something cute. This, along with an even tone and relaxed body stance, indicates that we aren't about to get hooked.

As foolish as it may sound, I suggest that parents who find it difficult to detach practice facial expressions in front of a mirror. We don't realize how our expressions give us away. Our mouths and jaws tighten, our eyes take on an exasperated expression, and our shoulders freeze. Learning to relax, smiling, or calling up the image of the toddler or inebriate in front of us are useful techniques in battling overreaction.

Distracting the child by asking a counter question can be extremely effective in detaching. "What makes you say something like that?" Or, "I often wonder why kids want to join Scouts and then don't want to do the projects. Why do you suppose that is?" Or, "I know. I used to feel like that before I grew up. I remember the time. . . ." When children are forced to listen to a parent experience every time they try to hook parents, the argument game loses appeal.

One of the most delightful responses to my request for shared parent wisdom came from the mother of a five-year-old:

"I twist a reply into such a complicated argument that I think Kelsey in her mind cries 'Uncle' and complies in order to stop the barrage. For example, Kelsey is very good about eating foods and trying things . . . because she is naturally so inclined? Nah! It's because I serve up sushi and before she can wrinkle her nose, I say, 'Kelsey, you gotta try this! People in Japan eat this all the time, and I thought it would be so much fun to go see the Tokyo Zoo, one of the great zoos of the world with animals you won't believe, but we can't go if you don't try things cause I have to make sure you won't be hungry and this is what they eat over there."

This mom added, "So, after browbeating my poor child with these peppy diatribes she now receives all new foods saying, 'Mom, where do I get to go and what animals will I see if I eat *this* food?'"

If a child is demanding a second reason after receiving a plausible first (and has three or four more on hold), a parent might say, "Why don't you go to your room and write down your reasons and I will study them? But be sure to use good penmanship and spelling because I want to be able to read them. I will reply to your reasons in writing. And then you can answer mine in writing and then we won't have to argue about what we said or didn't say."

One mother reported great success in having children write out their cases. It seems that every Sunday her pre-teens argued about having to attend church services, a non-negotiable in the family. She and her husband wearied of presenting the same reasons every week, so one Sunday she said, "I realize you aren't really hearing us and maybe we aren't hearing you, so this afternoon, instead of football or friends, we want you to write a paper on why you don't think church is important. We'll read it and respond to it in writing and then on Sundays from now on, you can just get out the paper and read it. That way we won't have to argue."

Children detest putting their reasons in writing. It takes the fun out of arguing and forces them to make sense. More often than not, they will simply end the argument with, "Never mind."

Parents can ignore non-verbal reactions without losing respect and authority. Learning to ignore non-verbal behavior and walking away is an honorable parent response to children's behavior. I emphasize honorable because many parents make huge issues out of non-issues like children's disdainful expressions, rolled eyes, and curled lips. Perceiving these as disrespectful, parents feel that if they ignore them, they will lose control.

More often than not, the opposite is true. When parents ignore children's non-verbal expressions, they defuse their power. Teachers learn this very quickly. Back in my teaching days, when I informed my sophomores that we were going to study poetry, I could count on groans, sighs, rolled eyes, and expressions of pure disgust.

The first time it happened, I tried to convince my classes that poetry was valuable and that they would come to enjoy it. They responded with more groans, sighs, and disbelief and I became more irritated. They had me hooked and knew it.

In years after that, I began by saying, "Get your groans and sighs in order because we're starting in on poetry." This defused their power and they ended up laughing instead of reacting. Or, more truthfully, laughing while reacting.

When parents perceive children's negative reaction as an assault on their power and authority, there's bound to be emotional stress and drained energy because children feel compelled to argue and test. When the very act of testing is considered disrespectful by parents, conflict becomes inevitable. Feelings are forced underground only to emerge unhealthily later on.

Basically, it comes down to the question, "Do children have a right to express anger?" If so, how are they permitted to express it without parent reprisal? If they are not allowed to argue or to disagree, they must resort to non-verbal techniques and if these are not permitted ("Don't roll your eyes at me, young lady." "Wipe that smirk off your face, young man."), they will eventually resort to sullen silence. And then parents are helpless because they cannot respond by forbidding silence.

It is when children, especially preadolescents and adolescents, go silent that parents seek help. By punishing all other forms of reactive anger, they've removed alternatives and just about insured a family life with uncommunicative children and adolescents who flee to the isolation of their rooms. When questioned by counselors, these baffled parents often insist that nothing occurred to initiate the teen's sullen silence. "Everything was going along fine," they'll say. "No disrespectful behavior or talking back or anything like that. But all of a sudden he stopped talking." These parents have to be led, often painfully, to acknowledge their role in contributing to their child's withdrawal by their own fierce need for respect and control.

The most effective technique to develop in dealing with children's non-verbal behavior is to ignore it. When we learn to do this, we gain rather than lose power and authority as parents. Ignoring it tells the child, "Your rolled eyes or sneer or impassive stone face don't affect me." We can walk away from the smirking child with dignity, commenting, "I'll get back to you later when you feel more like yourself."

Again, a steady tone of voice is essential. I am convinced that the majority of arguments arising out of children's non-verbal behaviors can be avoided if parents do not perceive them as threatening to their dignity, power, and authority. It is the parent who is most insecure who finds it difficult to ignore childish behaviors.

In a parenting seminar in Ireland a few years back, a mother shared a frustrating behavior of her thirteen-year-old daughter. "She's usually a lovely lass but when I say something she doesn't want to hear, she puts her fingers in her ears and sings, lah de lah, and dances around the room. It drives me wild. What should I do?"

"What have you tried that hasn't worked?" I asked, always my first question.

"I usually shout louder or try to pull her fingers away from her ears," she replied. "But it doesn't work. She just sings louder."

I turned the scenario over to the group of parents. "What can she try to stymie this behavior?"

Here are some of the group responses:

"She can do the same thing: dance with her and sing." This is a possibility and sometimes works but it can also heat up the interaction. Furthermore, many parents are reluctant to ape children's offensive behavior.

"She can continue mouthing words but stop voicing them." This could confuse the daughter or make her laugh, always a positive outcome.

"She could write any important message, hand it to her daughter and walk off." Right.

"She could wait till they were having a close moment and ask her daughter, 'When you behave like that, how do you want me to respond?'" Fine idea. It puts the problem back on the daughter's shoulders where it belongs.

"She can just smile and walk away." Clearly this is my option, especially if the smile is the indulgent kind we bestow on toddlers. I might even say as I walk away, "I'll get back to you when you're older."

Finally, one dad delighted the group by saying, "I would wait until she asked me for money and I would put my fingers in my ears and sing and dance around."

The mother who posed the question was thrilled. "I never thought of doing that," she repeated after each suggestion. She was eager to get home to try some of the proffered techniques.

However, one parent in the group objected to all the suggestions on how the mother should react, holding that it was the objectionable behavior of the daughter we should have been addressing. "I couldn't permit that behavior because it's so disrespectful," she said about the daughter's actions. "I believe she should be punished in some tangible way to get that unacceptable behavior stopped."

Her emotion-laden words initiated a discussion on the rights of and need for parents to establish behavior boundaries in the family. If, to some parents, the daughter's behavior is clearly unacceptable, they can establish a consequence: if you show disrespect by doing this, the following privilege will be taken away. Parents have every right to do so. We all need to set boundaries and these vary from family to family. What bothers some parents doesn't bother others.

The dilemma is that if the daughter's dance is a punishable offense, she may well resort to a stony face and sullen silence as an alternative and that isn't punishable. In truth, it is a much more difficult situation to handle than the finger-in-ears dance.

I prefer defusing, ignoring, even trivializing the behavior to punishing it. I believe changing behavior is more effective than disciplining it and certainly less wearing on parents. Yes, some behaviors deserve punitive consequences but many deserve to be ignored. When ignored, they are ineffective and rarely repeated.

When my children rolled their eyes at me, I learned not to react to their disrespect. I peered into their faces and said solicitously, "Do you have something in your eye?" Or admiringly, "You're doing that better today than yesterday." Or with wonder, "Where did you learn to do that? I would worry my eyes would get stuck that way." Or lightly, "Sometime I'd like you to show me how you do that without getting dizzy."

Such responses are not unkind but they have the advantage of allowing the child to show feelings while allowing the parent to react to them in non-confrontational ways. Basically, the parent is telling the child, "I know you don't like this request or rule but that's okay. You don't have to like it. Just carry it out."

When parents hassle over the same questions, complaints, and issues daily with children, change is necessary in order to achieve change. The Twelve-Step programs define insanity as repeating the same behavior over and over while expecting change. Any time a parent says, "I've told you a thousand times," it isn't working.

It's easy for parents to get into a frustrating repetitive dance with kids. The child complains, the parent responds in a predictable fashion, the child reacts to the parent's response in a predictable fashion, and so on. When the parent changes the dance step, however, and responds creatively and unpredictably, the child is forced to change the dance pattern. Let's look at an example of a familiar, predictable parent-child pattern of interaction:

Child: "I'll do it in a minute."

Parent: "I need it done right now."

Child: "I can't do it now. I have to finish this."

Parent: "Why can't that wait? Why do you always have to put things off?"

Child: "Why is it so important that I do it now?"

Parent: "Because I need it done now."

Child: "Well, I need to do this now."

Parent: (exploding) "How many times do I have to tell you I am tired of your procrastinating? You're not a productive member of this family. You expect me to do things for you on time but. . . ." And the battle goes on in the same tired fashion today as it did yesterday and will tomorrow with the same bleak results.

Let's assume that this parent sincerely wants change. She realizes that her predictable reactions aren't working and she's tired of the daily hassle. She garners her creativity and her courage and changes her dance step:

Child: "I'll do it in a minute."

Parent: "Okay. I'm setting the timer for a minute. Then I expect it to be done."

Child: Silence and no action.

Parent: "Minute's up and chore's not done. You know the rules. Turn off the TV. No more television or outside play until tomorrow."

Child: (wailing) "That's not fair."

Parent smiles and walks away.

Detach, detach, detach.

CHAPTER TWO

A Rule Without a Consequence Is No Rule at All

The Carson family rule states that children's phone calls are limited to ten minutes. Melanie has been on the phone fifteen and her father calls to her, "Time's up, Melanie." She ignores him and continues talking another ten.

"No more calls tonight, honey, " he says in a voice loaded with sympathy. "Sorry you did this to yourself."

"But D-a-a-y-a-d," she wails, "you talk longer than I do."

Recognizing it as a non-argument, he smiles empathetically and closes the conversation with, "You know the rules."

When parents express consequences but fail to carry them out, children assume all consequences to be negotiable. They become suggestions, wishes, or threats, not consequences, and lead to habitually argumentative children. For parents who find it difficult to stick to consequences, here are some basic guidelines to setting and carrying out rules, boundaries, and consequences.

Rules and consequences must be clearly expressed in advance of the conflict. In spite of parent disbelief, kids want limits, boundaries, and rules. They are uncomfortable with too much power. They want structure. They need to know just how far they can test before a consequence is applied. And they want stated consequences imposed if they exceed the limits. Otherwise they are confused and equate parent leniency with lack of caring. I've heard my own children say in reference to a child who has few rules and excessive freedom, "Oh, his parents don't care."

The more specific the rule, the better. Common family rules include the following: dirty clothes go in the hamper; no television until homework is finished; rooms will be cleaned weekly; children are responsible for putting away their own toys, shoes, books, etc.; chores before play; ten-minute limit on phone calls; and no hitting or verbal abuse.

Each rule deserves a stated consequence, i.e., it doesn't get laundered; no television; no fun until the room is clean; no further phone calls; if it isn't put away, *I* will put it away and *you* get to search for it; and if you hit, it's probably because television violence is rubbing off on you so, no TV for three days.

Many parents wait until they are in the middle of a conflict before they state the consequence and then it becomes a challenge: "If you don't, I will. . . ." Often it is said in the heat of anger and the consequence either doesn't make sense or it's too severe. When this happens, parents tend to relent and children get the message that consequences are inconsequential. I'd rather parents not state a consequence than fail to carry out the ones they state.

The manner we employ in asking children to comply or behave often determines a child's response. As parents we tend to order: "Empty the dishwasher." "Do your homework." "Pick up your toys." To a child, an order is an invitation to a challenge and children will almost always resist a direct order with a non-argument: "In a minute"; "In a while"; "I'll do it later"; "Why do I always have to do it?"

Substituting the simple phrase, "It's time to . . ." changes the request from a command to a statement. "It's time to get dressed," "It's time to stop that," and "It's time to get off the phone," are less commanding and less likely to hook resistance than outright orders.

When making a request of a child, the use of *when* instead of *if* also offsets potential confrontation. *When* implies a consequence without stating one—"When your room is clean, you can play." *If* gives children a choice, as in, "If you clean your room, you can go to the park." The child perceives this as an option and feels cheated if the parent gets angry when the child chooses to give up the park in lieu of cleaning the room.

More commonly, parents voice *if* negatively: "If you don't do this, you can't do that." Predictably, many children rise to the challenge with meaningless argument. By using *when*, parents remove the option while inferring the consequence: "When your homework is done, you can watch television"; "When the dishwasher is emptied, you can use the phone"; "When you've finished piano practice, you can skate outside." The children may still argue, of course, but the parent can smile and say in empathy, "Yes, it is a chore, isn't it? I am always relieved when my chores are done and I can do what I enjoy." End of argument.

We parents live with our own set of *whens*: "When we put in eight hours of work, we can go home." "When we work forty hours, we will get paid." "When we cook dinner, we can eat." "When we do the laundry, we'll have clean socks."

Even the most responsible parents, however, sometimes minimize or remove the very tasks that instill responsibility in children by taking on their kids' obligations. We shoulder their responsibility when we say, "Hurry up and finish your Scout project. Your meeting is in an hour." This informs children that completing their Scout projects is our, not their, responsibility. Far better for a parent to say, "When your project is done, I'll drive you to your meeting."

And what if the project is not completed? The parent can stick to the stated consequence of no project=no meeting, drive the child but force him or her to face the consequence of the leader's displeasure, or rescue the child by apologizing to the leader for the child's irresponsibility.

In our need to project our image as good parents, we often make the mistake of rescuing our children at the expense of our own mental health and pleasure in parenting. We spend enormous amounts of emotional and physical energy in taking on our children's responsibilities: prodding them to *their* practice on time, finding *their* carelessly tossed items, getting *them* up in the morning, nagging *them* to finish their homework, returning *their* library books, remembering *their* lunch money, and the like.

When we parents forget our lunch money, we face the consequences. When our children forget their lunch money and we rush their lunch to school, we remove the consequence from them. Far better for them to learn to deal with the consequences: a teacher's irritation, having to borrow food or money from friends, walking home for lunch, or, horror-of-horrors, hunger. Few children starve by missing one lunch. They may experience some hunger pangs, but they're not as likely to forget their money the following day.

Parental pride and guilt lie beneath much of our rescuing. We don't want to be considered negligent parents. We feel guilty if our child is the only one on the field without his uniform because he routinely forgets to pack it in his duffel bag. So we drive him back home for his uniform instead of allowing him the experience of being the only child out there in jeans and T-shirt. By doing so, we take away his opportunity to experience the consequence of his forgetfulness and to become responsible in the future.

A situation that frequently comes up in parenting workshops concerns the morning dawdler. "I call and call him," one mother said, "and then I nag him to hurry, dress, rush, eat, and find the things he needs. By the time he leaves, I'm a wreck." Her emotional energy is drained by 9 a.m., and she faces a full day ahead.

"Don't do it," responded a more confident parent. "Let him know you'll call him twice and after that, he's responsible for getting it all together in the morning."

"But he'll be late for school," the beleaguered mother replied.

"Let him be late," responded the second. "Don't write him an excuse. Let the teacher know you're trying to make him responsible and ask her to keep him in at recess for being late. It will put an end to his dawdling. It did with two of mine."

When consequences are clear and enforced, arguments dwindle in the home. When children realize they are going to be held responsible for the consequences of their behavior and misbehavior, they aren't as likely to spend endless time on placing blame and arguing which drains parental energy.

Setting logical consequences is difficult for some parents. As far as possible, it's wise to link the consequence to the act. If a child refuses to go to bed at bedtime, the consequence might be an earlier bedtime the following evening because "it takes you so long to get into bed and stay there." If a child creates a table disturbance, the consequence might be, "Take your plate and eat alone in the utility room. We won't permit you to spoil our family time together." If a child carelessly leaves his bike "somewhere," the consequence might be locking it up for a few days on retrieval, "to give you time to think about taking better care of it."

If he resists doing the dishes, a parent might resist cooking the next meal for him, forcing him to forage on his own. If she can't find her shoes, the parent might say, "Well, which do you want to wear to school, your slippers or your boots?" If an adolescent stays out beyond curfew, the parent can get him up earlier the following morning on the premise that the parent lost sleep worrying about him and thus needs his help in the morning.

If she dawdles and misses the bus, the consequence might be a day of ongoing chores at home—no fun, no television and no after-school play. If he fails to clean his room when requested to do so, the consequence might be that he can't use his room for a few days. If she doesn't pick up her toys, the parent might pick them up and stash them in the trunk of the car for a day or two.

Possibilities are endless. Sometimes in a parenting session, I present a list of children's offenses and ask parents to come up with logical consequences. They can be creative in groups but when they're alone at home, they tend to reach for the same tired consequences: no TV, no play, grounding. A little creative thought before the consequence is delivered can work wonders.

Some parents say, "I need some time to come up with an appropriate consequence to your action. Wait in your room without music until I think of one." The wait itself can be an instructive consequence to a child. Its discomfort might prevent a future wait outside the office of the principal, police officer, dean, or employer.

A wise mother shared, "When our children were older, we often asked for their input regarding what consequence would help them to do better next time." I like that better than our practice of having a child suggest three reasonable consequences and our choosing one of them, because her response indicates that consequences are learning experiences, not punishments.

Sometimes there is no consequence that can be logically linked to a given act or misbehavior. It's then that parents can withdraw privileges or service. Privileges that are often withdrawn include outside play, friends, phone, telephone, music, electronic games, one-on-one time with parents, or anything that's enjoyable.

Withdrawing service is more difficult for parents because they feel so guilty. I submit that when we are treated with disrespect by our children, we must allow them the same experience of feeling disrespected. "You don't seem to care about my wishes, so I want to let you know how it feels," we can say in a caring tone of voice. "I will not be driving you to your next soccer practice so you'll have to find a ride, walk, or miss it." Or, "I will not be cooking for you tomorrow. You can make your own dinner after we're done eating." Or, "I will not be reading you a story tonight."

Some parent-educators suggest that we ask for a "trade" at times like these—"I'll bring your project to school but then I won't have time to weed my garden, so you'll have to do that for me. Do we have a deal?"

Children quickly assimilate the message that family life is a cooperative affair with each of us contributing our share and interacting in a manner which benefits the whole family. When one member refuses to carry out responsibility or parental requests, that member is not entitled to the same reward and services that are awarded contributing members. Parents need to understand that if children continue to receive service-as-usual while treating parents with disrespect, they have no reason to alter their behavior. If, however, they feel the sting of withdrawal, they are likely to reconsider their actions.

A final word here concerns parent flexibility. There are times in all our lives when circumstances demand lenience, when rules and consequences should be bent. When a child is unduly stressed or ill, when there is over-stimulation in the family as at holiday time, or when events within the home—like a new baby or ill parent—create tension, wise parents realize that normal rules and consequences can be lightened or waived temporarily without permanent detriment.

It's good to remember that rules exist to serve the family, not the reverse. When we slavishly serve the rule, it becomes a tyrant, not an aid to easier communal living. Parents can bend rules occasionally without losing respect or control.

If the children's normal bedtime is eight o'clock but visitors want to enjoy the children, it's reasonable to let them stay up a little later than usual. Re-emphasizing the rule the following evening is likely to be necessary. The clever child will wail, "But you let us stay up later last night."

The clever parent will not argue. He or she will say in a pleasant, even tone of voice, "Yes, wasn't I wonderful? I sometimes am, you know. Now, it's eight o'clock and time for you to be in bed."

"Well, why do I have to go to bed at eight tonight when I didn't go until nine last night?" the child will persist.

Smile kindly. Say goodnight. Detach, detach, detach.

CHAPTER THREE

The Whys and the Whines

The small boy in front of me in the checkout lane at the supermarket grabbed a candy bar cleverly placed within his reach by marketing moguls. His mother stopped writing her check, turned to him and said, "Put it back, Eric."

"Why?"

"Because you can't have it."

"Why?"

"Because I don't want you to have it."

"Why?"

"Because it isn't good for you."

"Why?"

"Because it's loaded with sugar and sugar isn't good for your teeth."

The clerk folded his arms and rested against the back counter, waiting for her to finish writing her check. Those of us in line shifted impatiently.

"Why?"

"It makes your teeth bad."

"Why?"

"Because it puts big holes in them."

The man behind me moved to another lane. The "whys" went on interminably but finally the mother lost patience. She grabbed the candy bar with a shout, "Because I said so." The child set up a shriek which echoed after they exited the store.

The "why" child becomes one because it works. He doesn't want answers, he wants attention and/or an argument. And he wants what he wants! He will continue asking "why?" as long as the parent responds. Some children become so adept at the "why" game, they know just how long it takes to wear a parent down.

Responding to the chronic "whys" of children reduces parents to the point of anger more quickly than most other verbal behaviors. They know they are being manipulated but feel they must give logical replies, even to illogical questions. Eventually, like the young mother in the supermarket, they explode in anger, usually with a response they swore they would never use, "Because I said so." And then they feel guilty.

Parents are not required to answer every why. Once a logical response has been given to the child, the parent's responsibility is ended. Even if the child persists, the parent has the right to stop responding. "I don't know," "I haven't thought about it," "I've often wondered about that myself," "Hmmm . . ." or a smile are effective closures to the child's "why" litany.

Parents need to make a decision, however, on whether the "why" child is genuinely curious, doesn't understand, or simply wants to argue. Toddlers frequently ask "why" after "why" because they want to know. They believe parents have an answer for everything and are often disgruntled when parents can't supply an explanation. They can get downright angry when a parent says, "I don't know." To toddlers, parents are presumed to know everything and explain it in terms they understand.

But parents of toddlers have a tolerance point and if they sense it coming, they can say non-emotionally or with obvious sorrow, "I'm sorry. I just don't know. Maybe later." If the child persists, the parent knows it's an attention-getting device.

Three-year-old Jamie asks, "Why do bees sting?"

"To protect themselves against other bugs and people," his mother replies.

Jamie ponders this momentarily and asks, "Why don't dogs sting?"

"Because they protect themselves by growling or even biting," his mother answers.

"Why don't cats sting?"

Mother answers.

"Why don't elephants sting?"

Mother, realizing they are about to go through the entire zoo inventory, says, "I don't know."

"But why don't they?"

"I don't know."

"Why don't you know?"

This is Mom's cue that he's not interested in the answers but is playing the "why" game. Her response? Smile. Silence. Detach.

Older children often use "why" to question decisions rather than to understand the reasoning behind them. Parents can get caught up in endless arguments with adolescents who try to circumvent parental decisions by arguing peripheral issues.

Tom wants to go surfing with a group of older boys unfamiliar to his parents. They make a decision against his going. "We don't know these boys, and we think they're too old for you, " they explain to Tom.

"Why? What's wrong with them being older?"

"Nothing. They are the age they are and you are the age you are. When you are invited by boys we know and who are your age, come back and ask us."

"Why do they have to be my age? And why do you have to know them?"

"Because we care about you, and we don't want you to get into situations over your head with boys we don't know."

Although his parents have clearly stated their reasons, Tom could go on indefinitely with questions— "Why are the other parents letting their kids go, then?" "Why do you worry about me so much?" "Why don't you trust me?" "Why are you so strict?" "Why do you always think I can't take care of myself?" "Why do you have to make such a big deal out of everything?"

These are questions invoked to distract from the issue and to put parents on the defensive. Wisely, Tom's parents refuse to take the bait. "What is it about our 'no' that you don't understand, Tom?" his father asks. When Tom persists by ignoring the question, they simply smile indulgently and begin discussing something else.

For parents caught in the "why" game, here are some handy responses:

"I don't know. What do you think?"

"Seems strange, doesn't it?"

"Why do you ask?"

"I've often wondered about that myself."

"What does your 'why' mean?"

"I haven't the foggiest."

"I wish I studied that in school. Maybe you will
    sometime and then you can tell me."

"I'll have to think about that answer."

"I suppose there's an answer but I can't come up
    with it at the moment. Give me awhile to think
    about it."

"What an interesting question. I'd never have
    thought to ask it, so I'm afraid I can't answer it."

"I don't know but I'd like to. Will you look it up for
    us, please?"

"I don't know. It's *incomprehensible*. Can you say
    that word? It means I don't understand."

"The world is full of 'whys' I can't answer."

"Hmmm . . . that will take some thought. Don't you
    hate it when people give answers without thinking?"

"You know, I used to ask my mother that question
    and she didn't know the answer, either."

"Whys" are often accompanied by whines, which drive many parents batty. I am one of those parents. Whining was and is my nemesis, so much so that I developed and used this rule successfully with our three: *If you whine, you don't get it.* If they wanted a popsicle and their voices went up a half octave pleading for it, they lost any chance of getting it. "Too bad you whined," I'd say. "I might have let you have one otherwise."

If they were arguing with me about a chore or privilege and began to whine, the argument was automatically ended. "Oh, oh," I'd say, "I hear a whine. Argument's over."

Because whining was taboo in our home, I was astounded to hear one of my young ones go into a very accomplished whine at the home of one of his little friends, a professional whiner. I realized then that whining is situational, not inborn. Kids use it where it works and abandon it where it doesn't.

Whining is a manipulative technique which is effective with many parents. It becomes habitual in families where it is allowed and where it proves effective. Children who know they can hook their parents by whining will escalate their whining skills, moving ever higher on the whine scale.

Early childhood teachers tell me they can sort the whiners from the non-whiners on the first day of preschool. Since most teachers do not respond to whines, these children are confused because whining has always worked for them at home.

One teacher told of a four-year-old girl who was so accustomed to whining that it became her normal tone of voice. "She whined even when she was satisfied," the teacher said. "We had to teach her how to talk normally. But it confused her because when she went home, she reverted to a whine."

Parents do not have to succumb to the whines of children. We can treat whines as we might treat the use of four-letter words: they are not acceptable in this family. "Grownups don't whine," we can say (not entirely true, but they won't figure that out for awhile), "and we want to help you grow up."

One way of handling the whining child is to ignore him or her completely when the whine begins, coming to attention when it ceases. Since whining is most often invoked to get parents' attention, services, or treats, kids figure out quickly that it's counterproductive to their goal if they continue whining.

One dad who, like me, couldn't endure whining, set up a Whine Corner in the home. When children whined, they were "permitted" (sentenced) to sit in the corner and practice a different tone of voice for a certain number of minutes, then emerge and say the same words in a non-whine tone. "It really worked," the dad said. "Our Whine Corner collects dust now."

Sometimes children learn that behaviors that are unacceptable or ignored at home—temper tantrums, whines, endless "whys"—are effective outside the home. Parents who can ignore a tantrum in the kitchen will cave into it at the supermarket. Whining, absent at home, may suddenly emerge at Grandma's.

Children who practice this dual behavior have learned that parents are afraid of public scenes and will not confront manipulation and misbehavior outside their front door. Thus, the public sees these children at their worst because kids take advantage of their parents' discomfort in sticking to rules and boundaries when others are around.

How does a parent deal with this out-of-home misbehavior? By sticking to the consequences when they return home. Few of us will ignore a temper tantrum in the supermarket and most of us will cave in to children who see an opportunity to manipulate us and get what they want by embarrassing us in public. But if that child faces the same or stiffer consequences when she returns home, she will reconsider her behavior the next time she has an opportunity to go public.

One mother who struggled with this private/public dichotomy with her children said, "My children were not allowed to argue endlessly, to whine, or to say nasty things to each other at home so I was dismayed at how they behaved when we were at the homes of others. It was almost as if they were challenging us."

When she realized they were testing her rules and boundaries in public, she quickly terminated their public misbehavior by doubling the consequences once they returned home. If, for example, the consequence of whining at home was automatic denial of the request, the consequence for whining elsewhere was automatic denial of the next two requests. If kids continued to argue beyond acceptable boundaries in public, a double privilege was taken away as soon as they reached home.

So successful was her technique that she laughingly reported her children's reaction later on at witnessing another child's misbehavior at a restaurant. "Boy, is he going to get it when he gets home," they said.

Older children often utilize a more refined technique, that of making a snide or embarrassing comment about their parents in front of friends or relatives. "You should hear Mom when she gets mad. The other day, she . . . ." Or, "Yeah, Dad, tell 'em about how brave you were when . . . ." This is simply a more refined form of supermarket manipulation.

An effective parent response is to ignore it at the time and then let the child know that the next time he or she indulges in embarrassing the parent, the parent will respond by embarrassing the child in front of his friends. If parents follow through on their promise, it will happen only twice.

Stick to the rule, apply the stated consequence and detach, detach, detach.

CHAPTER FOUR

Springing the Anger Trap

"Yes, I'm an angry woman," Laura shouts at her husband. "Do you think I like being angry? I have to be angry to get any help around here. The minute I'm pleasant, everyone stops."

Parents like Laura get caught in a familiar anger trap. Instead of detaching or dealing with issues and conflicts in the early stages, they wait until they are angry before they demand a response. The result is that parents must exhibit ongoing anger in order to get children's attention. If they aren't angry, their kids don't take them seriously.

Worse, they discover they must constantly increase their anger level for it to remain effective. If a parent becomes angry over a child's untied shoelaces, he must become angrier over carelessly spilled milk and furious at outright defiance.

Contrary to some parents' belief, it's okay for parents to show anger. Sometimes anger is the only reasonable response to a given situation. When a child endangers herself or siblings, when there's careless and costly disregard for others' feelings or possessions, or when a child refuses to abide by parental decisions on important issues, anger is an appropriate and effective parent response.

In the recent past, parents were warned so strongly against displaying anger that conventional wisdom came to proclaim that *good* parents don't get angry. As a result, many of today's parents are afraid of showing anger. Even if they are seething inside, they keep smiling. Family therapists refer to this behavior as "the smiling stewardess style of parenting," i.e., remaining pleasant and serving even while being verbally abused. Children of such parents simply escalate their skills in testing these parents' tolerance level. The toddler in the supermarket serves as an example of the testing child.

Wise parents save anger for issues and behaviors which merit it. Overused, anger becomes routine and fruitless in changing behaviors. Parents caught in the anger trap might effect change by first asking themselves in a given situation, "Is this issue worth my anger?" Anger consumes enormous amounts of parental energy which can be better used in establishing acceptable behavior and preventing conflict so that there will be no need for anger.

I hear about the anger trap so often from parents that I've come to regard it as predictable. "I hate having to be angry but it's the only time my family hears me," one mother said. "They change their ways till I'm happy again, but as soon as I stop being mad they stop doing their share or start fighting again."

Frequently, parents who have experienced several hours or days of non-stop exposure to children—meeting their needs, listening to their arguments, and tending to a myriad of mundane tasks—feel resentment building up within themselves but they curb it until a final straw causes them to explode. That straw might be a child's remark, a torn shirt, or an empty ice cube tray. Then these parents react way out of proportion to the act. They may come tearing out of the bathroom shouting, "Am I the only one who knows how to replace toilet paper in this house? How many times do I have to tell you that the one who uses the last of it is responsible for replacing it? Why does it always have to be me? Do you think I'm your servant or something? Nobody ever cares about me. . . ."

Small wonder that her children look at her and think, "Weird." They don't understand the buildup of frustration.

They see only the final straw—an explosion over toilet tissue— and to them it's an inconsequential offense. Mom's overreacting again.

Parents who want to spring the anger trap need to make a concentrated attempt to express their feelings early, when they first feel resentment building within, so they can avoid the inevitable—and to children, meaningless—explosion of anger. A mother shared her technique for following such early intervention in a parenting class. "When I feel the first little anger seeping in, I stop and say to the kids, 'I'm starting to feel angry. Do you want to know why or do you want to wait till I explode?'"

I used a similar technique with different words to achieve results with my three.

"Do you agree that life is more pleasant around here when I'm happy?" I'd say.

"Yes," they would nod.

"Well, I'm not happy. Do you want to know why?"

More nods.

"Well, I'm unhappy because . . ." and I gave my reasons in a non-angry tone of voice. "Now, what do you suggest we do about it?"

Many parents report that when they explode in anger, they can't control their flow of words. "I become a historian," one mother said. "I dredge up every annoyance from the past and say a lot of 'You always . . .' and 'You never. . . .' Afterwards, I feel awful. How do we learn to limit our anger to current behavior?"

This is when verbal abuse usually occurs—swearing, hurtful name calling, etc. "You're a little _____." "You're just like your father/mother." "You'll never amount to anything." Such messages spoken in anger can create long-lasting and deep-seated self-doubt or even self-hatred. How can parents learn to restrict their anger to current behavior? It's difficult but possible if the parent really wants to set boundaries on his or her anger. While it's okay for parents to show anger, there are limits to be heeded. Attacking the child instead of the problem is destructive. An example:

Eleven-year-old Tim is constantly late for dinner. The family rule is that everyone will sit down together at six o'clock. The stated but rarely carried-out consequence is that if one is late without a good reason, he or she forfeits dinner. Frequently, though, Mom puts the family dinner on hold until Tim shows up, thus training him to be tardy, and then has to deal with complaints from her husband and hungry children. It's a no-win situation for her, and she pays in spent emotional energy.

This particular evening Tim saunters in fifteen minutes late. His hungry and tired father explodes. "So you finally decided to come home. You're disgusting. You never think about the rest of us. You always do what you want and the rest of us have to suffer. You're selfish. You only think of yourself." He sits down in disgust and the family eats in silence.

Dad has used his anger ineffectively by attacking Tim instead of the issue. Tim is wounded. He's chronically late and rarely receives more than a grumble. To hear his dad say he's disgusting and selfish is humiliating and enraging. He simmers in resentment, and wonders inwardly why he's being attacked for something as inconsequential as being late for dinner.

A more effective response, one still showing anger, would be for Dad to focus on the issue. "No food for you tonight, Tim. We've waited for you the last time. Maybe tomorrow you'll be on time."

Another useful technique in sticking to the issue and resisting the temptation to dredge up past offenses is to limit the amount of time parents use in dealing with a specific behavior. Some child psychologists suggest that any scolding that lasts more than a minute is counterproductive because kids stop listening and start resisting.

One therapist reported, "I tell parents that the essential message can be delivered to a child in a minute, so I attempt to teach parents two skills: to reduce angry reactions gradually to one minute and to allow themselves only three angry reactions daily. This can be rough on parents who start out by being angry all the time, but once they get the hang of it, these two rules become immensely freeing."

When parents control their impulse to harangue children over past behaviors and reserve anger for current behaviors, children learn to respect their anger. A ten-year-old said, "Mom gets mad all the time, so I don't pay much attention to her. But Dad doesn't get mad very often, so when he does I know I've really done something wrong. He doesn't yell or anything. Just says, 'I'm disappointed in you,' and walks away. I hate that."

We also need to recognize that parent anger begets child anger. Since children quickly learn to react to anger with anger, limiting parent anger to deserving issues makes sense. The parent who responds to minor annoyances with anger—"What's the matter with you? Can't you ever do anything right?"— is likely to hear angry retorts from children—"I didn't do it on purpose. Why are you always yelling at me?"

Eventually, these families disintegrate into an anger-based level of communication that becomes normal to them. Even "Come to dinner" is delivered angrily and so is the response: "In a minute." Such families are often unaware that there is an alternative voice available in interacting with one another.

We had a blessedly short experience with this kind of family years ago. They rented the home next door one brief summer and because both our families spent a lot of life in our fenced backyards, we heard their daily conversations. Everything was said angrily, even the most routine statement or question. Imagining the following conversation delivered in angry tones by even the youngest member of the family is helpful in understanding how anger-based communication becomes normal in families.

It's a sunny afternoon, and the children and mother come outside. "Who took my pail?" the five-year-old shouts.

"Nobody took it, Stupid. It's right there in the sandbox," replies her eight-year-old brother.

"Stupid, yourself. Where? I can't find it."

"You're blind, too. If you sat on it, you wouldn't know it."

"Shut up. Just because you're big, you think you're smart."

This continues awhile and Mom says, "Can't you two ever stop fighting? Do you want a whack or what?"

Dad appears. His wife greets him with, "So you finally made it home."

"Yeah. Why?" he demands.

"So call your mother. I'm tired of talking to her."

"What's she want now?"

"How do I know? She's your mother."

By now, readers have an idea of the emotional cost of living in an anger-based family (and living next door to one). At first, our young children listened with round eyes and whispered in fright, "They're fighting." Eventually, however, they shrugged and accepted the family communication next door as normal and even tried to mimic it in our backyard. Once.

This family was pleasant and polite while interacting with us but degenerated into nastiness with one another. Ironically, they had a poodle upon whom everyone in the family lavished attention and love. They would break off in the middle of a nasty comment to purr, "Oh, you sweet little pumpkin. You are the prettiest dog in the whole wide world."

Although we couldn't see them because of the solid fence separating us, we could always tell when they were talking to the dog by their tone of voice. One day, our young daughter said, "Why don't they talk to each other like they talk to their dog?"

"I guess they don't know how," I replied truthfully.

I really believe that. When families overuse anger, it becomes ineffectual and habitual. They don't know that there are more respectful and caring ways of responding to one another. Or that life becomes more pleasant when anger is used sparingly.

CHAPTER FIVE

Defusing With Humor

Terry, age seven, said, "I'm hungry, Mom. Can I have a cookie?"

"Afraid not, honey," she replied. "We're having dinner soon."

"But I'm hungry now," he grumbled.

"There are some carrot sticks in the refridge," she replied. "Grab a few of those."

"I don't want carrot sticks," he argued. "Why can't I just have one cookie?"

She detached and failed to respond.

But he persisted. "What's wrong with having a cookie? If I can have carrots why can't I have cookies?"

When she continued her silence, he screwed up his face and thrust his tongue at her. Startled, she stared at him and then began to laugh. "You look so funny when you do that. Here, come with me and look in the mirror."

Terry was confused. He wanted to stay angry but was intrigued over what made her laugh instead of becoming angry. He was caught in a dilemma. It's tough to pout and laugh at the same time.

Another parent, this one a dad, told of a time his wife was in bed with the flu. The children decided to prepare her a treat so they scraped the frosting out of all the Oreo cookies and rolled it into a single ball to present to her on a tray.

"I was ready to blow up when I saw what they did," he said, "but then I realized how funny it was and I followed them in as they gave this ball of gray frosting to my wife who hadn't eaten anything all day. She had to control a laugh and tell them it was a great idea but she couldn't eat it just then. We got a good chuckle out of it later but I could have blown it by yelling at them."

Stress-reduced parents look to humor as their first reaction to hassles. When I ask older parents to share with younger parents what they would do differently if reparenting their children, I usually hear this response: "I would laugh more and yell less. I wouldn't make big issues out of non-issues. I would enjoy the kids more and worry about authority less."

Humor is a valuable yet undeveloped resource in many families. Our first reaction to children's manipulation or misbehavior is usually exasperation, criticism, or anger, but we may be overlooking our most effective response in many situations when we ignore the humor in annoying situations.

When a child routinely looks at dinner and sneers, "Yuck. What is it?" we can react defensively with, "Look, I spent over an hour preparing this, and if you don't like it, tough." Or we can reply, "I'm not sure, but it was on sale."

When an adolescent objects to what he perceives as injustice because a younger sibling is treated more leniently than he remembers being treated—"How come he gets to do it when I couldn't at his age?"—we can try to defend ourselves, or say thoughtfully, "Well, when we saw what worked and didn't work with you, we decided to change tactics."

When a child wails, "But I *did* clean my room," we can put our hands on our hips and wail back, "You call this clean? Look at those clothes on the bed. Look at the stuff on top of your dresser. Look at your toys under the bed," or we can smile and say, "And what a job you did! Now I'd like you to clean it again while I watch so I can learn to clean as fast as you do."

When a bored child complains, "Mom, make him stop looking at me," we can play detective, umpire, and judge, grilling the offender who feigns innocence, or we can say, "And no wonder. We stare at people we love. So he must love you very much. Right, Cory?" That will get it stopped fast. No self-respecting sibling wants to be accused of loving his brother.

When a child rebels against wearing his boots in spite of two feet of snow outside, we can harangue about colds, discomfort and the cost of shoes, or we can say, "Right. I like to give options. I'll get you a couple of garbage bags and rubber bands instead. Then you can choose."

When a child who denies having homework (until the day before parent conferences, when the teacher routinely reports negligence) says, "I don't have any homework," we can spend precious energy interrogating him on his subjects one by one, or we can exclaim with enthusiasm, "Great. I've got some recipes that need recopying, and it will give you a chance to improve your penmanship."

When a teenager sulks and charges parental cruelty with, "All the other mothers . . ." or "None of the other dads . . ." we can retort angrily, "I don't care what the other mothers do. I'm your mother and you better like it, young lady," or we can agree sadly, saying, "I know. It's the luck of the draw, isn't it?"

When a child complains, "There's nothing to do," we can show exasperation and suggest endless ideas which are automatically rejected. Or we can show pleasure: "I've been hoping someone would say that because I need the plastic container drawer straightened. Please match the lids to the little plastic boxes and make it neat. Then, if you still don't have anything to do, see me because I have a few more things I haven't been able to get to." It's a good idea to keep these tasks in reserve— button sorting, penny counting, lint denuding, sock matching, toy repair, coupon clipping, letter to Grandma, etc.

When a chronic pouter pulls a face, we can react with irritation: "Go ahead and pout. Your pouting isn't getting to me," (she knows it already has or we wouldn't be reacting) or we can exclaim with delight, "That's a great pout. You've got your lip out farther than ever before. Do you think you can hold it until Daddy gets home?"

When a child mutters under his breath at one of our decisions, we can shout, "What did you say? I know it was something disrespectful. Out with it!" or we can remark, "You get three minutes of muttering and then on with the dishes," or, "I'm glad I'm not the only one who likes to mutter. Makes me feel better, too, when I can mutter about things I don't like."

The above are just a few examples of situations that are potentially explosive but can be defused with a bit of lightness and imagination on the part of parents. In addition to preserving parental energy by defusing non-arguments, humor also presents a model of reaction to children who must deal with conflict at school, in play, and at Little League. They learn how to react from their parents, and if they're fortunate in having parents who can deal with conflict with occasional humor, they are likely to follow suit.

To be effective, humor must not be unkind or overused. Like anger, humor can be overused. If parents always respond with a funny quip, it generates anger in children because they feel trivialized. Because humor is unanswerable, it can lead to greater child anger. Some issues and situations lend themselves to a humorous response while others do not.

For example, if a child claims unfairness, not as a parent-baiter, but as a genuine issue, it is inappropriate for a parent to respond with a funny retort. Although we may be tempted to respond in fun, we must be careful to reserve humor for issues that deserve it. We have lots of choices when it comes to responding: ignoring, sympathizing, agreeing, discussing, psychoanalyzing, and apologizing. Tossing a humorous response in now and then makes a nice change of pace, but it can be overdone.

More deadly is the misuse of humor—humor that is unkind. I've already discussed sarcasm, but teasing, put-downs, and trivializing also heat up rather than defuse family conflict. Teasing can be cruel, and it leads to a habit of family teasing. Often it generates deep anger in children, anger which emerges in unhealthy ways later on.

Few of us like to be teased out of a mood or away from an issue serious to us, if not to others. When someone says, "Oh, come on. Don't you have any sense of humor?" our blood pressure rises. When we tease an unhappy child with, "Let's have a smile," or "Here we go again. Poor, poor little Danny is sulking," or we tickle him to make him laugh when he wants to cry, we're abusing humor, not using it.

I often suggest families utilize a tease list which is respected and posted. Family members, mom and dad included, are invited to list three things about which they hate to be teased and the family will honor them. The list can be revised periodically but it keeps the family aware of its responsibility toward the happiness of all. What seems innocuous to one member is often hurtful to another.

When nothing comes quickly to the tongue, keep in mind that humor is only one of several approaches available to parents. For example, there's one handy response to children's non-arguments: "Because I love you." It can be said with a variety of inflections:

Serious: When a child fights cleaning up his face, hair, language or behavior, we can say, "Because I love you and I want others to see how lovable you can be."

Empathetic: When a child objects to a routine rule, we can say, "Yes, I know. Sometimes it's hard to live with people who love you, isn't it?"

Exasperated: "I wish I didn't love you so much. It would be a lot easier to deal with this. But (sigh), I'm afraid I do." (second sigh).

Humorous: "Because I love you. That's my problem, I know, and I'm working on it. Meanwhile, bear with me."

And when the child retorts, "You sure have a funny way of showing it," we can agree and ask for help. "You're right. How would you show love in a situation like this?"

And when he replies, "By letting me go," we can smile and say, "Maybe I won't love you so much someday, but right now . . . (drift into silence) . . . I promise I'll work on it."

It's hard to argue with parents who tell you they love you, but they're working on it.

CHAPTER SIX

Negotiate, Negotiate, Negotiate

Fourteen-year-old Mark belongs to an army of early adolescents who subscribe to the philosophy, "Why get B's when you can get by with C's (even though you could get A's)?"

His parents, understandably, believe otherwise. Knowing Mark's abilities, they expect him to earn A's and they inform him of this—constantly. They nag, scold, harangue, and ground him while he, in turn, ignores, argues, and procrastinates.

The three of them are locked into an ongoing dance of conflict which affects the family mood negatively. Dinner time has become an unpleasant rehash of Mark's class-by-class progress. He resents the grilling and reacts in stony silence. When privileges are withdrawn, he shrugs and withdraws into himself or his room.

His parents are distraught and frustrated. They've tried everything—reasoning with Mark, meeting with his teachers, sticking to consequences—but results are always temporary. After a brief period of improvement, Mark slips back into his C pattern.

Mark's poor school record stems not from parental disinterest but from the fact that his standards and expectations differ from those of his parents. Getting A's is simply not that important to Mark, who is at an age where he feels he has a right to his own, not his parents', goals and expectations. He views their standards as an attack upon his independence and integrity.

When they warn him that he will not get into college on C's, he says, "That's okay with me," or "That's my problem." When they scold him for a poor test grade, he just smiles sardonically and says, "Guess I'm just not very smart." Even when they praise a good paper or grade, he reacts negatively.

Like many fourteen-year-olds, Mark is a pain in the parental neck a good deal of the time. He's flexing his independence muscles by challenging his parents' right to impose their expectations on him. With Mark, it's grades. With others his age, it might be friends, clothing, hair, or music. As tough as it is on parents, Mark is behaving normally for his stage of development.

At his age, the push for autonomy intensifies. Parental rules and expectations are viewed as challenges to his independent self. Even if Mark wanted to earn better grades, he might deliberately slack off because he knows his school success is important to his parents, and he can use average grades as a weapon in his struggle for independence. The more important the issue to the parents, the more powerful the weapon in the hands of the adolescent.

If parents don't care that much about academic achievement, adolescents will test some other issue dear to parents: appearance, religion, fitness, athletics, or interests. So how can parents deal with the issue of expectations and standards while respecting the individualism and development of the child?

It's important that parents realize that they have a right to set minimum standards and that children have a right to negotiate these standards. In Mark's case, there's no room for him to negotiate because his parents have set maximum standards as minimum. He realizes that getting B's instead of his usual C's won't satisfy them, so why try?

If his parents admitted, "Mark, we're concerned about you because we love you and care about your future, but what we're expecting isn't working and it's making all of us miserable," he's apt to listen. If they add, "How can we negotiate your grades so we're both happy?" he might be the one who says he'll get a B average if they stop demanding A's.

If he doesn't offer this concession, however, they might say, "We aren't going to continue to nag you because we realize your grades are your responsibility. But setting minimum standards is our responsibility. We know you can get A's but we also know you're content with C's so how can we negotiate this?"

If he's unwilling to negotiate, they can say, "Fine. Maybe when you're a little older you'll be able to negotiate, but for now it looks like we'll have to set the standards. We expect a B average. If you slip below that, outside school fun will be curtailed until the next grading period."

If they stop nagging and stick to their standards and consequences, he will soon realize that he, not they, is responsible for his achievement. They *must* stick to their stated consequences, however.

I repeat the rule: parents have a right and obligation to set minimum standards, but often those standards are too high, especially with firstborns. I set unreasonably high standards with our eldest but quickly learned that the perfectionism I demanded of her was counterproductive to her self-image and to family harmony. When, through experience, we lowered our standards with our sons, arguments and conflict diminished.

Parent perfectionism can be a curse in families. When we expect the home to be in perfect order, the children to accomplish tasks perfectly, and life to proceed as we've ordered it, we're asking for conflict. We need to understand more about child development. Often, children aren't capable of achieving the perfectionism we demand. Their small or large motor skills aren't developed enough to button their shirts correctly or write as legibly as we like.

They also view standards differently than do adults. Is there any parent among us who, after scolding, "I told you to clean your room," hasn't heard a child respond in indignation, "But I *did* clean it."? How clean is clean? I doubt that parent and children will ever agree on that one.

There's a humorous saying that bears a great seed of truth for perfectionist parents: "One way to meet our expectations is to lower them."

If we want to do away with ongoing arguments on the clean room, we need to learn to negotiate with children. With my sons, I stated my minimum standards: "If there are no clothes on the floor and no dirty dishes or mold-growing food, I won't hassle unmade beds, clothes on the chair, or toys and papers strewn around." They agreed to it, and I had to keep my end of the bargain, even though it was tough to remain silent at times.

Their rooms, after all, are *their* rooms. And they have a right to their clutter if they like it. When their room gets untidy enough or when they need to find something, they will straighten it.

On a personal level, I note that the standards I hold for the rest of our home are lower in my office because it's mine and how I keep it is nobody else's affair. I confess to keeping an untidy office. A casual observer might look at the piles of papers strewn from file cabinet to table to desk to computer console and pronounce it chaotic.

But I know where everything is and I don't want to take the time to even the edges of every pile of clippings, manuscripts, letters, and papers. If I want a certain letter or piece of information, I go directly to that pile and search for it. Granted, nobody else could, but they don't need to.

I would resent it deeply if my family came into my office and declared, "Look at this room! It's a disgrace. Look at those piles of papers. I want this place cleaned up immediately or there will be no telephone tonight."

We can diminish arguments by learning to negotiate with children on standards. Even the youngest child is capable of negotiating if we give him or her the opportunity.

We can ask, "Which toys do you want to pick up and which two do you want to leave out?" Or, "Which two television programs do you want to watch after school?" Or, "Do you want to play first and then do your homework or do your homework and then watch television?" Or, "Which room do you want to clean, the kitchen or bathroom?" Or, "Do want to peel the potatoes or make carrot sticks?" Or, "What time do you think you should get in tonight?"

If the adolescent says 2 a.m., we can smile and say, "I see you're not old enough for this (an insight they hate) so I'll set the time." The next time, the offspring is likely to come up with a reasonable time or negotiate one. He may want to stay out till twelve while his parents want him in at eleven, so eleven-thirty might be a reasonable compromise.

Parents who negotiate realize that eventually children are going to leave home and make all the decisions regarding their daily lives: when to get up, when to put themselves to bed, how to budget money, which courses or job to take, how to behave on spring break, how long to go without doing laundry, and when/if to clean their room. If young adults have no input in making decisions at home, they are going to be at a disadvantage when they're on their own.

Jim and Kathy McGinnis, co-founders of the Parenting for Peace and Justice Network, are strong advocates of the family meeting, a practice in which all members have input discussing and resolving issues. They tell about the time their son, Tom, put "cable TV" on the agenda and then delivered "Twenty-seven reasons why our family should get cable TV."

> ". . . he gave back to us all the values we had expressed over the years dealing with television, lifestyle, family togetherness, fairness. He had figured out how we could get cable TV without spending any extra money (part from the children's allowances and $8.00 a month from us if we would stay home with our children and watch a TV movie together instead of going out to a theater). No additional TV would be watched (we have a limit of seven hours a week), but probably better TV (movies instead of some of the prime time violent shows all three children were attracted to). He gave us his twenty-seven reasons, then sat back down and looked at both of us.

"We were a little shell shocked to say the least! We all agreed to give it a try, even though we had told him only the day before that he was wasting his time putting cable TV on the agenda because we had said 'no' to that only six months earlier. He had genuinely spoken to all our values and found a way of incorporating them into his proposal. More than any other single event, that has convinced us of the value of family meetings as a way of sharing our faith and values with our children."

Negotiation implies a loss of power to many parents but that's what parenting is all about—gradually moving from total power over the helpless infant to sending independent young adults out into the world. To achieve this, we start relinquishing power and responsibility to young children and encouraging independence and responsibility as they mature. Giving children a voice in the simple decisions that affect their daily life does away with a lot of potential argumentation.

One mother shared a great idea on curtailing non-arguments over food likes and dislikes. She invites each child to list three disliked foods and she posts the list on the refrigerator. When she serves these dishes, the child is not obligated to taste or eat them but is allowed to make herself a sandwich instead. This gives the child some power in food struggles and diminishes arguments because the mother simply says, "Why not put it on your list next month?"

One of my sons went through a stage where he rejected everything I served at dinner. He greatly enjoyed my irritation and became quite polished at folding his arms, staring me boldly in the eye and saying, "I don't like that."

Finally, I said to him, "I know you don't like most of the meals we serve but you do like hard-boiled eggs. So from now on, I want you to come out before dinner, look over what we're having, and if you don't like it, peel yourself a couple of eggs. I will keep some boiled for you."

He thought it a great idea and he ate hard-boiled eggs for three weeks. Then, one evening, he ate formerly-spurned meatloaf. His older brother, unable to let it pass unnoticed, said, "I thought you didn't like meatloaf."

"I don't like eggs anymore," he replied. From that time on, he partook of most family meals without complaint.

Giving kids options, even if parents choose the options, is always helpful in offsetting arguments. We aren't losing authority but sharing power and responsibility, which go together. Learning to negotiate isn't that difficult and once parents experience it, they realize how effective it is in establishing smoother relationships in the family.

Besides children's inability to attain them, overly high parent standards can become counterproductive by discouraging shared responsibility in the family. Often, we ask children to take on a household task and then criticize the results. Parents, especially mothers, complain about not getting help, but frequently their spouses or children report, "She's never satisfied with the way I do it." *Wise parents praise the effort, not the results.* Even if the standards are not up to their expectations, they learn to accept lower standards in exchange for more shared responsibility in the home.

I liken it to a fictional situation in which a husband with a bad back asks his wife to clean the garage for him. She does and then he appears in the doorway and inspects her efforts and remarks, "You put the hammer in the wrong place. And those trash cans should be aligned. And, how many times do I have to tell you that . . . ?" What are her feelings at this point and how eager is she going to be to help next time?

In spite of old family scripts clogging our consciences, everything we do isn't worth doing well. Perfectly-sewn Halloween costumes, elaborate color-coordinated child birthday parties, floors so clean you can eat off them (Who wants to, anyway?), homes devoid of toys, books, and other amenities lying around, manicured lawns, immaculate garages . . . who says we must subscribe to this definition of healthy family life?

Quite simply, parents who overcome perfectionism within themselves and lower their standards enjoy their children more and their children enjoy family life more. They argue less about how clean is clean, how a better performance could or could not have been achieved, or what the neighbors might think. By negotiating standards and responsibilities together, they are then able to waste less energy arguing and waste more enjoyable time together.

In an earlier chapter, I mentioned that I frequently ask older parents what they would change if they had an opportunity to reparent their children. One predictable response is, "I wouldn't sweat the small stuff."

"And what is the small stuff?" I ask. They list kids' rooms, food struggles, clutter, children's appearance, athletic scores, and all A's.

As one who struggled with perfectionism in my young parenting years, I know how costly it is to family comfort. I learned that things will be misplaced, mistakes will be made, children can go to school in outlandish outfits of their own choosing without my being considered a negligent parent, and that the lived-in look in our home and yard doesn't mean we'll be rejected by our neighbors.

A forty-year-old in one of my parenting seminars put it well, "We had a messy home, but a neat family. My best friend had a neat home and a fussy family. I was the lucky one." Most of us would agree.

CHAPTER SEVEN

Home: Haven or Havoc?

The Talbot family was in turmoil, not because of parent/child tension but because their thirteen and sixteen-year-olds were at each other's throats. They weren't squabbling over issues but over the very existence of one another in the home. When the two were together in a room, their mutual antagonism was so palpable that it affected the mood of the entire family.

One evening after a particularly unpleasant family meal, they breached their mother's patience point and she commanded, "Get your jackets. We're going for a walk."

They stared in disbelief. No way were they going to be seen with their mother and each other, they said. "This isn't negotiable," she said firmly. "You are making life miserable for the rest of us, and we're going to walk and talk until you get whatever's bugging you out of your systems."

They headed for a local trail where they couldn't be seen by cruising friends. Setting a rapid pace and placing herself between them, Mrs. Talbot said, "The rest of us don't know what's going on between the two of you but you're going to get a chance to get it out *now*." Turning to one, she said, "You get to talk about your sister as long as you like and we won't interrupt. Then she gets to talk about you as long as she likes and we won't interrupt. And then you get to talk again and then she gets to and so on. When you both get it all out, then I get to talk."

Call it therapy on the hoof, but it worked. Resentments poured out. Each accused the other of self-importance and deliberate attempts to embarrass the other. Each felt the other was diminishing his or her status to win favor in their parents' eyes. Each dredged up hurts and humiliations from the past and forecast worse for the future. Each couldn't abide the way the other dressed, ate, talked. Some of their allegations were so patently absurd and unfair that their mother was hard put to keep from interrupting.

The teens spewed forth for nearly an hour. Finally, they tired of it and said they were ready to quit.

"Now it's my turn," Mrs. Talbot said. "You said some pretty hurtful things and if you didn't mean some of them, I hope you'll tell each other later when you're getting along better. But you needed to say them and to hear them. That's why we're taking this walk."

She explained that sometimes when friends and spouses feel hurt or unloved by the other, they don't tell each other the real problem so it shows up in little things like cutting remarks, snubs, and silences. They looked at her as if this was a new idea, so she expanded on it a bit, realizing that it helps to lift an issue out of the immediate situation and discuss it in a neutral third-person situation at times.

Ultimately, she said, "The rest of us can't change how you feel about each other or us. That's up to you. Maybe you'll like each other someday, maybe not. That's your right to decide. *But your right to unpleasant behavior ends when it starts affecting us, and right now you're making life very unpleasant around the house. You don't have to change your feelings, but you do have to change your behavior or spend your life in your rooms. Now, can you handle this or shall we set up a schedule of certain times when each of you can be with the family and the other is in your room?"*

Grudgingly, they said they could handle it, and they did. There was some backsliding, but their animosity gradually diminished and family harmony was restored.

Parents have a responsibility to take action when the ongoing behavior of children affects the family mood. Often parents ignore this responsibility, hoping that the tension will evaporate on its own. Or they deal only with symptoms like increased fighting between children. But unless steps are taken to address the root of stressful situations, the tension usually escalates.

In recent years, business managers have focused much attention on the environment of the workplace, recognizing that productivity is directly related to stress experienced in the daily work life of employees. When the work environment is conducive to positive staff interaction, productivity increases. When work dissatisfaction is high, however, productivity diminishes. Employees become irritable, lethargic, and competitive instead of cooperative.

So it is in the family. As a society, we have focused on relationships within the family but paid scant attention to the *environment* of the home in which the family interacts. Yet, it's difficult to establish close and caring relationships in a strained or chaotic environment.

Many of us have had the experience of visiting homes and families with dramatically differing environments. I'm not discussing cleanliness, size, furnishings, and factors related to income but intangibles which nurture a climate of peace or disharmony. One can almost feel the environment of a home upon entering. An atmosphere of comfort and relaxation assails the visitor, or, conversely, a sense of tension or chaos spurs the visitor to flee as quickly as possible.

In the past, home has been sentimentally described as "a haven in a heartless world," and it often was. Life was arduous and cruel in the coal mines and mills. Home was an escape from work and world, a place of hearth, peace, and comfort.

Paradoxically, today we find people escaping home for the peace of the workplace. For many whose homes are tension-filled conflict centers, the peace and structure of the work world bring relief. Instead of finding home a haven, many find it a hassle with excessive chaos, demands, and stress. While they may long for a haven, their home environment is so far from being a haven that they seek it elsewhere.

One mother put it bluntly, "I need to go to work for peace of mind. When I'm home I'm constantly arbitrating, commanding, arguing. My office is heaven compared to my home."

I find her words exceedingly sad. Home should be a place to escape to, not from. I asked her to name the major differences between environments at her home and office. She said, "At the office, everyone knows the rules, does his or her job, and treats the others with respect. We can laugh together and we help each other out when one is behind in their work. It isn't that way at home. Nobody seems to care about rules, responsibility or respect. It's a relief to get away. I guess you could say we love each other, but we don't much like living together."

Research indicates that this mother has lots of peers—men, women, teens—who feel similarly about their home environment but also feel powerless to change it. They seek their havens elsewhere: work, church, fitness centers, shopping malls, pubs, clubs, or in other relationships.

In most of this book, I focus on children's behaviors and parent responses, but in this chapter and the next I will examine the backdrop of family life which underlies, nurtures, and determines behavior. When the environment is conducive to discord, negative behaviors increase and parents must work harder on dealing with the fallout. When parents are aware of and promote the intangibles that lead to a positive family environment, potential hassles diminish.

In this chapter, we'll look at mood and order, and in the next, at noise level, activity level, and courtesy.

Mood

I mentioned earlier that all families operate within a mood. While moods fluctuate in daily family life, depending on temporary stresses, most families operate on a basic mood range between pessimism and optimism, noise and quiet, conflict and harmony, and chaos and order.

Some families remain generally upbeat even while experiencing conflict and setbacks while others retain a normally pessimistic mood even when things are going well. What accounts for the difference? Chief among determinants is the parent's or parents' attitude toward life in general. When parents are hopeful and positive in their outlook toward others, work, and world, children absorb this attitude and model it in their daily lives. They perceive setbacks and conflicts as normal and surmountable. They are able to shrug off their own and others' human failings and they look for the positives in failures.

Conversation tends to be more positive than negative: What good things happened to us or in the world today? What do we look forward to? How do we support each other in upcoming activities? This is the family that really means it when they ask, "Did you have a good day?" or "How did your game (or test or presentation) go?" It calls a meal of leftovers a smorgasbord and it doesn't degenerate into self-pity when weather cancels a picnic but, instead, pulls out a deck of cards or tells ghost stories on the family room floor in the dark.

In families of this sort, conflicts exist but are handled swiftly and forgotten rather than rehashed. Parents tend to speak of relatives, co-workers, and neighbors in a positive light, sharing their strengths rather than their defects. Negative news reports are often followed by, "Well, one good thing about all this is. . . ."

In my work on stress within military families, I note that families who operate within a positive mood are those who adjust more positively to a transfer. Even when the parents dread assignment to what they perceive as "bad duty," say a fictional post named Camp Cahoots, they don't share this sense of dread with their children. And if their worst fears are realized, they don't complain about drawing the short card but, conversely, announce, "Wonderful news! We're going to Camp Cahoots! We get to play in the wind and see the biggest sandstorms in the country. Won't it be great?"

They pull out maps and tourist guides and prime their children for experiencing a new life. They take advantage of the fact that children's adjustment to a new environment is directly related to the parents' attitude toward the same.

Positive attitudes build cheerful environments. The result of optimism is that parents and children alike tend to see the world and life as pleasant places to exist even though they experience problems. They aren't beset by fear and despair but live with hope and confidence that together they can handle what comes along.

What a huge gulf exists between the positive family and the family on the opposite extreme, the one whose normal mood is one of negativity! The pessimistic family focuses on blaming rather than solving, on complaining rather than communicating, and on anger rather than conciliation. Its conversation centers on what's wrong with school, work, playmates, the neighbors, and the world.

A typical conversation goes like this: "Did you hear about the shooting over on Sixth Street?" "Yeah, but what can you expect of people who . . ."; "All politicians are corrupt"; "It's a jungle out there . . ."; "Don't trust anyone"; "Teachers get paid too much."

An ongoing diet of negative conversation leads to depression, which explains why some families exhibit symptoms of chronic depression in their daily environment. Back in the sixties when America was in the throes of depression over Vietnam, race riots, and protests, psychologist Bruno Bettleheim wrote in partial explanation of children who were dropping out of school and society, "We send our children to school to make their way into the system and then we tell them the system is lousy." The result, of course, is that children give up and drop out. Who wants a piece of such hypocrisy?

Negativity can destroy the spirit. One woman told of how the family was adversely affected by her husband, a chronic pessimist who distrusted everyone. "One morning I looked out the window after a snowfall and saw our neighbor shoveling our walks. I called to my husband and children, 'Look, Tom is cleaning our walks. Isn't that nice of him?' My husband walked over, looked out, and said, "Humph, wonder what he wants.' It took the spirit right out of me."

The good news is that negativity can be turned around because it is habitual, not natural. Babies are not born negative but become that way through exposure to environmental pessimism. We tend to take on the mood of those around us but we have a choice in accepting or rejecting it. We can change or leave a depressing conversation, turn off negative news channels, refuse to get engaged in pity parties and discourage gripe sessions by remaining silent.

For families who find their mood more negative than positive, I suggest they focus first on becoming aware of negative behaviors and simply begin calling attention to them, perhaps by saying, "This is getting depressing. Did anything good happen to anyone today?" or "If you don't mind, I'd like to switch the news off. It's getting me down."

When a deliberate effort is made to offset a depressing environment, family members are usually cooperative because we're all seeking a haven at home. Even if children are too young to understand, they intuit the mood and respond to it. When parents are positive and content, children tend to follow suit, and when parents complain, children tend to whine, argue, and fight. Then parents have to deal with the negative behavior. It makes more sense to deal with the environment that produces such misbehavior.

The example of the feuding siblings illustrates this point. Initially, the parents spent precious energy on dealing with the teens' negative behavior, but nothing changed. When the parents focused on how the teens were affecting the family environment, change occurred. The parents had to be entirely prepared to isolate the teens from the family because they were eroding the climate in which the rest of the family lived. The teens had shifted the family mood from pleasant to unpleasant in an incredibly brief span of time.

Mr. and Mrs. Talbot found themselves asking, "What's going on here? Why do we have to feel depressed and oppressed because the two of them choose to be hostile? Let's take steps to get it stopped—just let them know that if they can't be part of a comfortable family climate, they can't be part of the family at all."

When the parents took action, teens understood that they weren't going to be permitted to contaminate the home environment and changed their behavior, allowing the parents to cease the wearying discipline. Mrs. Talbot reported, "I believe they were relieved when we stepped in with a rather drastic solution because they weren't enjoying living in the midst of a hostile hassle any more than we were. They just didn't know how to get out of it."

Another factor in creating a positive family mood has to do with those little tangibles that create cheerfulness. When fiction writers want to set a dreary mood, they mention bleakness, darkness, damp, lack of color, stuffiness, and cold. When they depict a happy scene, they mention flowers, fresh air, color, hearths, laughter, and warmth.

What makes a home warm even when nobody's at home? Children's paintings on the refrigerator, plants scattered around, family photos and mementos. It is clean and uncluttered, but "lived in." These are the tangibles that make stable living infinitely more pleasant than temporary existence in a basement flat or military barrack.

Sometimes, in our fast-track lifestyle, we neglect the simple amenities that enhance the soul. Plants require care, flowers wilt and have to be replaced, bright colors soil more easily than dull ones, windows take time to open and close. Few of us want to return to the days where the odor of fresh bread baking was considered essential to a comfortable home, but it is helpful to look around with a stranger's eye occasionally and ask ourselves, "Is this a cheerful home? Does it show life or does it resemble a hallway? Do those of us who live here feel uplifted upon entering? Does it seem dark? Dreary? Does it feel stuffy? Is the music jarring or soothing? Are the odors offensive or welcoming?"

A workplace environmental engineer told me once that the first thing he observes in visiting a large office complex is the use of color. He shared an interesting insight. "I find that when color is used on the walls, and in the carpeting and furnishings, the employees tend to dress more colorfully and exhibit more liveliness. When I visit an office where everything is beige and wheat, people dress in beige and have personalities like wheat."

That may seem a bit extreme, but the little extras in a home make a difference. If we have drawers full of pretty place mats but don't take time to use them, it's easy to progress to filling our plates at the stove and taking them to the television set. That's not what healthy families do to create a warm atmosphere.

I remember a scene from an outdoor marketplace in Europe in 1960. I watched housewives with their mesh bags carefully shopping for produce from stall to stall, scrutinizing vegetables and bargaining for the best prices. It was obvious they were on a tight budget and they shopped accordingly.

However, almost every one of them made a last stop at the flower stall and purchased a small bunch of fresh flowers. I recall this vividly because it intrigued me. Flowers were a luxury to us (and we were far more affluent than the women at the marketplace appeared to be), but to them they were as essential as the potatoes and cabbages they bought. Since then, I've come to understand and appreciate that there's more to creating a home than meat and vegetables.

Order

"They keep an orderly home." How often have we heard that accolade or one similar to it? Order is frequently misunderstood, however. To some, it signifies predictability and comfort, while others view it simply as regimentation.

Order is just another word for structure in the family. *Rules and rituals*, the two components of structure, foster smoother living among individuals, whether it's in the workplace, army or family. When rules and rituals are absent, chaos reigns. There are no set times in daily life for rising, eating, playing, working, studying, and retiring. There are few rules, and the ones that do exist aren't enforced.

In homes that lack order, parents aren't sure where their children are or when they'll be home, and children aren't sure where their parents are or when they'll be home. Other children, sometimes unknown to the parents, wander in and out of the home. A woman reported that she was in the bathroom at her sister's home when a child walked in, ran a glass of water, and turned to stare at her.

Unnerved, she asked his identity and her sister replied, "Him? Oh, I don't know. Just one of the neighborhood kids, I guess."

The chaotic family spends a lot of time looking for things. Children, clothing, and sports equipment appear and disappear, and so does the family car. Nobody's sure who has it or for how long. Schedules are rarely logged. Children announce school needs or practices at the last minute, and the family responds chaotically.

A social worker described a typical chaotic family. "You're sitting in the kitchen with the parent or parents, and children come in, get into the refrigerator and cupboards, eat what they want, spill milk, knock over a chair, and the parents say nothing because they don't even see it."

My son spent a year as counselor in a shelter for troubled preteens. In conversation, he shared with me some of the rules imposed on the twelve teenage boys living there. When they made their beds before breakfast, they earned a point. When they showered without resisting, they earned two points. When their homework was completed prior to classes, they earned three points and so on.

At the close of dinner each evening, points were tallied and they were awarded a certain number of telephone calls, television time, and outside sports based on points earned.

I listened with dismay and said, "Doesn't that seem terribly juvenile? The kids are practically teenagers."

My son responded patiently, "You don't understand. Most of these kids have never experienced structure in their lives. They haven't lived with even the simplest rules. We have to begin as if they're toddlers and teach them structure. Most of them end up liking it because they can trust a structure here that they've never had before. Where they suffer is in returning home to normal chaos."

I'm not suggesting that highly stressed families are like the home of these teens or that parents should set up a point system like the one used at the shelter. God forbid! We would spend more time in bookkeeping than parenting. I share the example only to indicate to parents how valuable simple rules and rituals are to the emotional and behavioral well-being of children and parents alike.

All healthy institutions require rules. The reason a new school or job is stressful for a period of time is unfamiliarity with the rules of the new environment. When a friend inquires about our adaptation to new surroundings, we find ourselves saying, "Once I get the hang of it . . ." or, "We're finding our way around." In short, we're learning the rules that govern the new experience.

Let's imagine for a moment a workplace that is run like a family without rules. The office manager scurries from desk to desk every morning urging, "It's time to start work. Stop dawdling and chatting." He spends the next couple of hours policing his work force: "You spent too much time on that personal phone call." "Get your feet off the desk. It doesn't look good to clients." "I've told you a thousand times to save your computer stuff every ten minutes." They roll their eyes, argue with him, and tell him, "Get real."

It's coffee break, and the office manager has to announce it, time it, and herd employees back to work. He has to oversee everyone's responsibilities because he can't count on their meeting them if he isn't there. Whenever he leaves the office, they stop working, and start goofing off. By noon he's exhausted and still faces four more hours of the same.

How long would such a manager last, either professionally or emotionally? He would be replaced within a week by a new manager who would win the respect of his employees by stating the rules, sticking to them and firing workers who refuse them. That's the consequence of refusing to respect leadership and authority.

"Fine," I can hear parents mutter. "How do we fire kids?" By stripping them of their "salary"—their privileges. The Talbots were prepared to fire their two teens by banishing them to other rooms until they were fit to have around. We have to communicate to children that our rules are serious and enforceable and that removal of privileges and service is the cost of defying family rules.

Arguments drain parents, but rules take the argument out of issues. Little rules make life easier. It's as simple as that. If there's a family rule that everyone picks up his or her dishes at the end of the meal and carries them to the kitchen counter, it becomes automatic after initial resistance. Parents don't need to get into that exhausting exchange:

"Come back here and clear the table before you watch TV."

"I did."

"Your bowl is still there."

"That's not my bowl."

"Yes, it is."

"Yeah, but I didn't use it so I shouldn't have to clear it," etc.

Rules, like anything else, can be overdone in the family. Where there are too many rules or they're too restrictive, there will be rigidity coupled with rebellion. But families with a comfortable environment adhere to some minimum rules: if it's to be laundered, it goes in the hamper; no television until homework is done; call if you're going to be late; tomorrow's school paraphernalia will be laid out tonight; parent permission must be sought before a friend is invited to dinner or to stay overnight.

Rules will vary from family to family but one thing is clear: healthy families possess rules and honor them. Their rules are clear but flexible. If a child starts arguing over having to don mismatched socks, parents need not get defensive but empathize, "I'm sorry you forgot to put your socks in the hamper. I'm afraid I already did laundry this morning." And they say no more. The rule speaks for them.

If a child asks permission to see an early television program after dinner, the parent says, "Of course, as long as your homework is done." If the child continues to plead, the parent simply smiles and detaches. Arguing takes the energy out of parents, but rules take the fun of arguing out of the kids.

Rituals differ from rules, but are immensely valuable in creating a comfortable home environment. Although we tend to think of candles and incense when the word ritual is invoked, family rituals are more commonplace and mundane. Rituals are repetitive actions that become automatic in daily life. There are few rules governing them. They come into being on their own.

Most people have a ritual upon rising in the morning. Perhaps they brush their teeth, then put on coffee and radio, then dress, then call the children, and then feed the cat before picking up the newspaper from the front doorstep. They don't follow this ritual because there's a rule that they do so but because it takes the decision-making out of their early morning life. They don't have to weigh their minute-by-minute schedule each day anew. They may not even recall making the coffee or their drive to work.

If, however, their morning ritual is disrupted by oversleeping or a phone call, their automatic pilot switches off. They have to think and make decisions on how to catch up. The morning disruption raises their stress level and consumes precious emotional energy better spent elsewhere. Their break from ritual finds them arriving at school or work frazzled, and it can affect their whole day.

Most family rituals come into being without planning. In truth, when parents hear children say, "We always do it that way," they are often surprised that what they thought was a one-time occurrence has become a ritual.

When our family took our annual summer trek to visit Grandma, my husband and I were bemused at how quickly the unloading and reloading of the car became a ritual. The first evening that we did so, each child carried certain bags and paraphernalia into the motel. After that, each day they wordlessly reached for the same load as if they had been assigned to it. This pattern went on for years, whenever we vacationed.

Family rituals are as simple as everyone's taking a specific chair at the table. No energy is wasted over choosing, arguing, and voting before each meal on who is going to sit where. Where muddy shoes are deposited, who goes first, second, and third into the shower in the morning, and what family members do when they walk in the door from school or work are all rituals. Do they shout, "Hi, I'm home!" or do they wait for someone to discover them? Do children check in with mom or dad or simply head for the refrigerator? Do they dump everything on the dining room table or take it to their rooms?

Lack of ritual indicates chaos, as in the family where the mother reported, "Most of the time when our children's friends call and ask if they're home, I have to say, 'I don't know.'"

I note that some families tend to have a lot of rituals which they fall into naturally. I watched mesmerized while visiting a brother's home years ago. I shared a routine evening meal with him, his wife, and their five school-aged children. When we finished eating, everyone sat until my sister-in-law rose to pour coffee for the adults.

With a *whoosh*, the five children jumped up and began to clear the table. Apparently, coffee signaled the beginning of their after-meal ritual. As we adults sipped coffee, I watched the children execute the fastest cleanup I've seen—and all without a hassle or word.

One rinsed the dishes, one put them in the dishwasher, one stored the leftovers and condiments, and one cleaned counter, stove, and table surfaces. The final and youngest of the five dampened a paper towel and walked about the floor wiping up spills and spots. "We call him the spotter," my sister-in-law explained when I remarked upon the scene later. "That job has always belonged to the youngest because he's the closest to the floor."

Within eight minutes, the kitchen was clean and the kids were outside playing. They learned that they could get in more play time if they didn't stop to argue with each other and their parents. The same kind of ritual was repeated the following morning as they dressed for school and when they returned home from school.

My brother and his wife saw nothing noteworthy about these rituals, but rather assumed all families operated with them. Some of their children's actions began as rules, they explained, but gradually became part of their daily ritual.

And that's what parents can strive for if they want to reduce the hassles and arguments in daily family life. When rituals become second nature to children, order and harmony reign, but when rituals are absent, the result is disorder and havoc—a fertile breeding ground for family conflict. When our rules become so ingrained that they become rituals, meaningless hassles disappear.

CHAPTER EIGHT

A Kinder, Gentler Home

Noise Level

A young child who began turning down invitations to play at a friend's home explained his reasons to his parents. "I don't like it there," he said. "It makes my tummy noisy." Further questioning revealed that the noise level in his friend's home upset him to the degree that his stomach hurt while there. He may have chosen a peculiar expression but his connection between noise and stress was right on target.

Many of us have shared his experience, not in homes, maybe, but in buses, malls, and even recreation areas designed for leisure. Noise levels have escalated in our culture to the point that when we don't hear music, traffic, or background talk we're vaguely uneasy.

Our collective tolerance for noise has expanded in tandem with increased volume through technology. Music designed to soothe has given way to music that jangles the nerves. "Special sales" are noisily announced over store loudspeakers, urging customers to buy more. Electronic game palaces can be heard a block away, and television sports announcers view even three seconds of silence as deadly to ratings.

At the same time, we spend a lot of money trying to combat rising noise levels by use of carpeting, acoustic tiles, and even little machines that sit on the desk and emit something called "white noise," noise designed to mask other background noise. What absurdity!

Noise level tolerance varies in families. Some live comfortably with stereo, radio, and television playing at high volume simultaneously, while others consider any one of the three jarring. However, parents who are able to accept a high noise level are often surprised to learn that it correlates with family stress: when the noise level is consistently high, family stress is usually high, as well.

Of course, children are naturally exuberant and noisy, especially in play. We've all been in situations where excessive frowns over children's normal play noise moved us to exit as quickly a possible. A "hushed-whisper" environment is no place for children. Noise doesn't have to be abolished but it needs to be controlled if a peaceful family climate is the goal.

To put it simply, *parents have a responsibility to monitor the noise level in the home.* What is excessive noise? Children and parents are unlikely to agree on the definition of excessive, but when we find ourselves having to speak more loudly than normal in routine conversation, we're living with excessive noise. When background noise of children's play, television, or stereo grates on *anyone* in the family, it needs to be moved, turned down, or turned off. If parents are constantly asking children to lower the volume because they can't concentrate or talk, the volume is excessive, in spite of the kids' protests.

Parents can't control personality traits, interruptions, or weather, but we can control the noise level. If "Turn that down," is part of our hourly litany, we need to look at some new rules. One that many parents use effectively is, "We'll ask you to turn it down once. The second time we'll ask you to turn it off." And they act accordingly. They enforce the stated consequence and then detach.

When two or more teens want to play their stereos simultaneously, and the home sounds like a rock contest, this is the time to switch to earphones. Another often used rule is that when visitors come in, television goes off. If someone is in the middle of an important program, and their TV can't be moved, then the visit should be moved to another room, or porch, or patio. It's discourteous to viewers and visitors alike to attempt conversation in the midst of television noise.

Voice level also correlates with the family noise level. Families who want to reduce the stress level might concentrate first on reducing their collective speaking volume. When parents speak more softly, children lower their noise level as well. I learned this lesson when I had laryngitis as a teacher. As my voice dropped to a near whisper, my sophomores followed suit. I was tempted to make it a chronic condition!

The voice level in the family increases proportionately to the background level of music, telephone, and television. "They don't talk; they yell," remarked one grandfather on his son's home environment. His wife tried to defend their son with, "Well, they have to yell to be heard over all that noise."

Activity Level

"Fast-track," frenzied," and "over-scheduled" are familiar adjectives used in describing family life today. So involved are individuals in their own lives that the family calendar becomes the new hearth. "I get home after my son leaves for work, and I'm barely in the door when my daughter rushes in from basketball practice to change for her church youth group," a father reported. "My wife is waiting somewhere to pick up our youngest from his practice, or Scouts, or something. I wouldn't mind if this kind of thing was a sometime occasion but it's normal. Like living in a circus."

He spoke wistfully of a more relaxed home atmosphere, but seemed to feel that a frenetic schedule was inevitable. Many parents relate to his feelings and disappointment. They feel helpless in trying to find time to sit down together at any time during the day. Weekends are filled with games, appointments, and errands, and when Monday rolls around they are happy to return to work, exhausted by the coordination of everyone's needs and activities. "Hurry up," becomes the operative phrase in the frenzied family, and it sets the mood for pressure. Wasting time together in the family is a lost dream. Usually, such parents give up trying, and the family comes to resemble a collection of roommates in a rented home.

Friends and colleagues of ours from other cultures who have spent considerable time studying in America always mention the activity level of family life as one of the most incomprehensible and disagreeable aspects of American life. To them, our need for the plethora of outside activities is pathological, not laudable. A common observation among foreign visitors is that we have lost the meaning of family by escaping into activity. "Families here don't seem to want to spend time together," a foreign sociologist remarked. "It's rush, rush, rush. Where is the time to enjoy what you work so hard to obtain?"

Sobering words. Families do not have to capitulate to the philosophy that holds that the best parents have their children signed up for the most activities or that they themselves must relinquish their dreams of a relaxed home simply because other families are doing so.

The healthy family puts some controls on the activity level of children and adults alike. A common rule is that each child is permitted to take part in one outside activity requiring practices or projects during a given season. If it's a sports league, he doesn't have time for Scouts. If it's ballet, she doesn't have time for gymnastics.

If they're always rushed and rarely have relaxed time to spend with the family, parents, too, must accept that they need to limit their outside clubs and hobbies. If parents work eight hours daily, they may have to choose between a quilting class and aerobics, or between a bowling league and weekly poker. I have often discouraged parents with at-home children from volunteering for church or community activity if both work outside the home. There will be time for that when the children leave. This is the parents' chance to spend unhurried time with their children, and they won't get a second chance.

"How do we know if our activity level is out of control?" parents ask. Here are a few clues. If parents find it difficult or impossible to arrange a get-together with relatives or friends for several weeks ahead, the family is over-scheduled. If family members resent a visit from a treasured out-of-town relative because of their activities, they're overscheduled. If "hurry up" is the most oft-repeated phrase, the family is overly frenzied. If parents and children find themselves trying to accomplish two or more things simultaneously—cooking while on the phone, correcting papers at the soccer match, working on the computer while helping a child with homework—the calendar is out of control.

Most telling, if there's an environment of ongoing hurry-and-pressure, the family is stressed, not healthy. This stress sets up conditions for conflict, short tempers, fatigue, and argument. Parents may find themselves wondering why they're living the way they do and yet feel they're too busy to take steps to control their lives. Activity replaces the very deep values for which they are longing—peace, intimacy and shared unhurried time with those they love most.

Courtesy

Courtesy and politeness indicate the presence of respect in a family, and respect is one of the top five traits found in healthy families. Researchers who study family interaction often invite families to be videotaped while solving a problem, so that they can observe their own interaction later and, perhaps, change some of the communication techniques.

Intent on solving the assigned problem, families who agree to the taping don't realize that the courtesy or discourtesy they display toward one another is being scrutinized as fundamental to their problem-solving skills. Often, when families view the tape of themselves interacting, they are dismayed at the number of interruptions or put-downs, as well as the absence of polite responses like "please," "thank you," and "sorry."

"One cheap way parents can make life better immediately is to begin saying, 'please,' to their children," an experienced therapist remarked. "Imagine what would happen if, all over America tomorrow, parents agreed to say 'please' and 'thank you' every time they ordered a kid to do something. Kids wouldn't know how to act. Why do parents ignore such a simple device?"

I can't answer his question, but I agree with his words. Lack of courtesy leads to disrespect, and when we feel disrespected within our own homes, we are devalued. Many of our arguments and conflicts spring from anger at feeling devalued. We do not feel devalued when we are treated courteously.

Many families live by a simple rule: *we will treat each other with courtesy at all times.* Courtesy, or lack of it, becomes habitual. It's interesting to reflect on how a couple who treat each other with respect and even reverence before marriage gradually drop simple courtesies and replace them with unthinking or hurtful behaviors after marriage. Sometimes it's simply a matter of efficiency. It takes less time to say, "Get the car keys," than "Will you get the car keys for me, please? Thanks." Courtesy takes time but it's a good family investment because it pays off in a more harmonious atmosphere.

Families who are interested in reducing arguments by improving their home environment will do well to become aware of their courtesy level. How often do they express the big three: "please," "thank you," and "I'm sorry"? Commands diminish respect. Polite requests imply respect. Corporate managers have become aware of this simple truth in the past couple of decades. Employees treated with respect are more loyal and productive in the workplace. The same holds true in the home place.

One mother, responding to my request for reparenting wisdom, wrote, "What I wish I'd done that I didn't (on the false assumption that a sense of duty would be eroded) was to thank the kids for all they did." The work ethic defeats its own purpose and dampens the spirit when it manages "Good job," but gags at "Thank you."

Other parents find it difficult to say, "I'm sorry," to their children when apologies are in order. They fear that apology signifies weakness. Yet often these same parents expect their children to apologize freely. Apology doesn't signify weakness, but rather regret over a behavior or misdeed. Saying to teenagers, "I'm sorry I forgot to give you your phone message," enhances rather than diminishes children's respect for a parent. It tells them their parents are human with human fail-ings and feelings. If, on the other hand, a teen is angry over missing an important phone message because of a parent's for-getfulness, and the parent disregards or devalues the anger, the teen feels trivialized and anger is sure to follow. It's simpler to say, "I'm sorry." And to mean it.

Interrupting is another form of discourtesy in the family. We should note, however, that not all interrupting is disre-spectful. In my research on healthy family communication, I found that families who communicate interrupt more than families who do not. What is important is to recognize the dif-ference between respectful and disrespectful interruption.

Some families adopt a style of short-hand conversation in which members freely interrupt because they grasp the gist of the other's words and the interruption indicates they don't need to finish. Long-married couples exhibit this practice even more dramatically. They converse in a series of half-sentences: "Do you think we should put the key—?" "Yes, they'll proba-bly be late—" "But if the rain—?" "But then they would—" and so on. This truncated communication drives outsiders batty, but it works for some families and is not considered dis-respectful because it is the family's style and everyone is equally interrupted.

Disrespectful interruption occurs when there's an imbal-ance, that is, when some people in the family are never inter-rupted and others, particularly the youngest child, are always cut off in mid-sentence. This creates frustration and anger in the person trying to be heard. It tells her that what she has to say simply isn't as important as what others have to offer.

Some children become elective mutes when they've been cut off so many times. They simply stop trying to communi-cate. Others explode in anger, thus igniting further family con-flict. If parents find themselves constantly saying, "Let her finish," or "Stop interrupting," they might examine their own habit of interrupting. If they themselves rarely interrupt, how-ever, then they need to set up some consequences for those who do and stick to them. "When you next interrupt, we'll let you listen for five minutes."

Another discourtesy is the failure to acknowledge and greet someone's presence. An older visitor to our home surprised me once by saying, "I like coming here because your children always say, 'Hello' when they come in. Do you realize how rare that is?"

I didn't, because I was reared to search out and greet my parents when I came home from school and always to greet visitors to our home, whether I was in the home when they arrived or they were there when I entered. So I simply passed on the same behavior to my own children.

Social skills like courtesy and respect must be modeled and patiently taught by parents. Children who are lucky enough to learn them in their home have an advantage in adult life over those who may have more education but fewer social skills, because these social skills are necessary in relationships, the workplace, and the larger world.

Since my friend's comment, I have noted the validity of her words. I have been in many homes where I was neither acknowledged nor greeted by the family's children. It's unsettling.

It's not only children who are guilty of this discourtesy, however. As parents, we need to greet playmates of our children just as we would greet our friends so they feel welcome to our home. Sometimes, parents wonder why their children always play at a friend's home, but friends rarely play at their own home. Children have an intuitive sense of being welcome or unwelcome in a home, especially if their presence is ignored by the grownups there.

Many other discourtesies too numerous to discuss fully here abound in families. Common ones include playing music too loudly for the comfort of others, prying into others' mail or rooms, eavesdropping on phone calls, leaving a mess for others to clean up, monopolizing the TV remote control or changing channels while others are viewing, borrowing without asking, failing to help when another is in stress, using the last of anything—ice cube, toilet tissue, gas—without replacing it, and invading others' solitude or turf. The list is endless in some families, but it ends in those families where action is taken to eliminate common discourtesies.

The foregoing, then, are a few of the basic components of any environment. At one time, the workplace was a noisy, colorless, forbidding kind of place where employees spent an unpleasant eight or ten hours and then escaped home for comfort. Hospitals, churches, and schools were essentially the same. When attention was paid to the environment, these institutions became more comfortable.

When we experience conflict in the family which produces ongoing argumentation, we tend to focus on individuals and ignore the environment that fosters the misbehavior. All families might benefit from doing an "environmental study" in order to identify both the factors that increase the havoc and the factors that help to create a haven known as home.

CHAPTER NINE

Sharing the Wealth

In this chapter, I am sharing ideas and responses from over 200 parents who attended my workshops or who wrote in response to an article I wrote on creative parenting. After reading the shared wisdom, readers will, I suspect, be as grateful to these parents as I am for taking the time to share their techniques, ideas, and humor.

Some parents wrote comments at the bottom of the form. "I hope you can get some ideas from these. I used not to be so flip and curt with my answers, but I have three teenagers and you quickly learn to be a bigger smart aleck than they are and come up with quicker answers," one wrote.

Another penned, "My mother told me you have to keep ahead of the kids. Heck, I can't even catch up with them."

Here are a few of their parenting tricks.

In a workshop designed to help adults lighten up, I invited parents to bring a favorite toy of their own. One young mother fascinated us by executing intricate loops and rolls with a yo-yo. She explained the origin of her skill. She keeps it in her jeans pocket. When her children pester, argue, whine, or fight, she takes it out and begins playing with it, giving it her full concentration. When she first did this, the kids continued to argue, but now they realize her attention is no longer on them and as soon as she reaches into her pocket, they drift away.

In the same workshop, another mother displayed a well-worn puppy hand puppet. She uses it whenever she faces a disagreeable scene with the kids, letting the puppy speak for her. She demonstrated how she wakes her stay-in-bed son with the puppy. She nips at him and nuzzles him, saying in a puppy voice, "Get up. I want to play. It's time for our breakfast." The boy buries his head deeper into the pillow, but the puppy burrows, too. Finally, her son cries out imploringly, "Make him go away, Mom." Mom's not the mean ogre—the puppy is.

Having leftovers for dinner usually generates groans and complaints. A mother wrote that Thursday is leftovers day in their home. It's known as MDO—Mom's Day Off—and the rule is, "No complaining about food on Thursdays." During the week when someone complains about the food, she says, "That's okay. Maybe it will taste better on Thursday." Or, if they like the food, she cautions, "Hey, careful. We don't want to go hungry on Thursday." They aren't required to eat the leftovers, but no snacking is allowed between Thursday's dinner and Friday's breakfast.

My friend, Ann, devised an ingenious plan for using leftovers. Soon, in fact, her children's little friends begged to be invited to "Foil Packet Dinner." During the month, Ann made single-serving packets out of leftovers and tossed them unlabeled into a basket in the freezer. When it looked as if there were enough for a family meal, she heated them in the oven and served them on a large tray. Each person took one, opened it, and either kept it or passed it to the left. It could be anything from peas to pizza to peach cobbler.

The rule held that anyone could take and eat what was passed on to them, but if the packet made the rounds and came back to the original owner, he or she had to eat it without argument or complaint. Ann's children are grown now but when they visit, they ask for Foil Packet Dinner.

A woman named Ellen wrote, "When my children charge me with being mean, I respond, 'I learned that at Mean Mom School.' I elaborate with, 'Every new parent is required to attend. I had to go once a week for six weeks to learn all this, etc.' If you get on a roll, the kids actually end up laughing."

Another woman wrote, "The most annoying question my three children asked was, 'What can we do?' I'd suggest chores, but they'd rephrase it to, 'What can I *play*?' Because I'd usually suggest one idea after another only to have them turn it down, I finally made this rule.

"I'd give three suggestions. If none was acceptable, they had to come up with their own, and they were not allowed to ask that question again that day.

"Suggestions I remember giving them: play 'office' with the used envelopes and mail I'd saved; play 'library' with our books; play 'gas station' with bikes and water from hoses as gas; play 'supermarket' with cans and boxes of extra food stored in the basement."

A colleague of mine, upon reading this anecdote added, "I have a friend who'd respond to this type of question with some ideas and the last idea was always, 'or you can mope around wondering what to do.' A description of the current behavior was always the last choice."

I hit upon this one by accident but it came to be my favorite tool to use in the 'I'm bored' or 'There's nothing to do' frustration. One day our normally creative and active daughter told me she was bored. Because it was so unlike her, I said, "You must not be feeling well. Get the thermometer, please, and we'll check it out." She didn't have a fever, but I had her lie down for an hour, anyway. Her experience was noted by the other kids and it quickly did away with "I'm bored," because they knew I'd say, "Get the thermometer," and order a rest.

On the same topic, a mother wrote that whenever her children complained that there was nothing to play, she assigned them to put on a play for her later in the day. They weren't given the option of saying no. "I told them their play was their responsibility and my work was mine. When they tried to hand their responsibility over to me, I told them that they had a choice of doing my work or putting on a play. It put an end to their boredom complaints, and I saw a few rare plays."

Summer nightmares? Listen to this mom.

"At the beginning of each week during the summer, I put a list of activities on the bulletin board for the week. The kids have to do two a day from the list, which includes both chores and pleasures. If they do all the fun things early in the week, they know the end of the week is going to be a bummer. A typical list might read like this:

Weed the flower bed.
Draw a cartoon or comic strip about our camping trip.
Clean the bathroom.
Make popsicles.
Clean your room.
Call Grandma and talk to her alone.
Straighten up the plastic bowl cupboard.
Invite a friend to go swimming.
Sort out the sports equipment and shoes.
Play with Mom's old makeup.
Clean up the inside of the car. Vacuum and wash windows.
Put up tent in backyard and sleep out.

Sometimes we can over-negotiate and over-explain. One mom shared her experience on learning this. "We always felt it was important to give a reason when we said yes or no to our children. One of my favorite responses came from our fourteen-year-old daughter who said, 'Mom, before you say yes or no, please just a yes or no—not a long drawn-out explanation.'"

In one of my parenting seminars, a dad contributed this bit of wisdom. "We go to a lot of these workshops because we want to be more knowledgeable parents. We've found we usually pick up just one idea that sticks with us and helps a lot. Seems silly, I know, but those 'one ideas' have been invaluable in disciplining our kids. The three most valuable were:

1. It's okay to tell kids they hurt our feelings or that we depended on them and they let us down because kids *should* feel guilty when they are guilty. We shouldn't worry so much about making kids feel guilty.

2. Instead of focusing on what a kid did wrong, focus on 'How do we keep this from happening again?'

3. Instead of charging in and accusing kids of misbehavior, which usually heats up the situation, use these techniques: 'It would be helpful if _____'; 'Some people find it helps to _____'; When you _____, I get _____ because _____'; 'I expect _____.'"

And, from another parent, "Our kids always argued over who had to sit over the hump in the back seat of the car and who got to sit in the front seat. I got tired of hearing, 'I sat there last time,' so I put a notebook and pencil in the glove compartment and made it the responsibility of the hump-sitter to write his or her name and date in the hump column and the name of the child sitting in the front seat in the front seat column. If there was an argument, I just said, 'Get out the book and look.'

Since they usually neglected to write it down, they had no argument. Eventually, they quit arguing."

"My husband came up with a winner to keep peace and love as our family increased in size," wrote a reader of my weekly column. "He began with our first two who got into the habit of bringing complaints about each other to the dinner table. Their father, in a firm voice, informed them that each one must relate at the dinner table something nice about the other that occurred that day. This ritual continued throughout the years. If he didn't ask right away, we could see them squirming in eagerness to tell their 'nice.'"

A grandmother offered, "Two of my five great-granddaughters live next door to me and are with me part of each day. They are now four and five. When they began whining at age two, I told them I didn't allow 'whiny cats' in my home or on the property. I told them to throw the whiny cats away—I was allergic to them. They know I am allergic to cats. Each time they whined, we went through the same routine. They would throw the whiny cats away. Soon they stopped whining."

I visited my friend, Julie, at her daycare center one day. As we were standing talking, a five-year-old came up to interrupt. Julie simply put her hand up and the child waited a few seconds and then went off to play. I remarked on her action later and Julie explained that her "halt" gesture means, "Wait until I am finished talking and turn to you." She said that the children know that if it is urgent, they may break into the conversation, but if it isn't urgent and they break into it, she will ignore them.

She also uses the technique to put an end to argument. "I look away and put my hand up. I don't engage in eye contact with them at all when they just want to argue. They learn quickly that it's useless to argue when I look away and put my hand up."

What a simple but workable solution, especially for parents whose children rush to interrupt during phone calls or when there's a visitor, or for parents with children who just want to argue.

Julie also commented on the tantrum-in-supermarket frustration. "The problem is caused by inconsistency on the part of parents. Sometimes they cave in to the child's demands, sometimes not, so the child is certain to intensify efforts to get what she or he wants. I tell my parents that the best solution is not to take them next time. Smile sweetly and say, 'You're not ready. I'll take you when you're ready.'"

We had two rules on high school grades, chores, and driving. We tried to make the link between grades and driving by saying, "Anyone smart enough to drive has to be smart enough to get a B average. So if your grades drop below that, we'll curtail your driving until you bring them up." We had only one quarter when we had to enforce the consequences, but we knew our son was testing us. After driving to school, he hated taking the bus again and worked hard to get his grades back up. (Before anyone sets this rule, be sure your child is capable of a B average. Otherwise, use a C average or whatever the child is able to reasonably achieve.)

The other was a chore-linked rule we enforced during the pre-driving years: *Anyone who intends to work a car has to prove he or she can first work a washer, dryer, vacuum, range, lawn mower, and other household equipment.* It worked beautifully for us.

A friend's six-year-old was fearful of going into her dark bedroom alone because she was told by older children that monsters lurked there. After much futile reassuring, my friend told her daughter that if she said, 'Booga, booga,' before she went in, monsters would flee. It worked and the family reported much delight in hearing a brave little voice echoing down the hall, 'Booga, booga, booga,' as they sat in their living room.

We also had monsters in our family, except that they resided in the closet of our three-year-old Dan's room. He slept with his seven-year-old brother, Pat, who probably suggested the monsters' presence in the first place. Dan began awaking nightly in real distress. We turned on the light, opened the closet door, reassured him, and sat vigil by his bedside until he fell back to sleep. One week, though, I noticed that his nightly traumas had ceased and commended him for his courage. "Oh," he said, "Pat shot them."

It was more effective by far than all our psychological efforts.

A final monster solution came from a dad: "When our daughter started fearing monsters, we bought a spray can of air freshener which I covered with adhesive paper, pictures of monsters and the words, 'Monster Spray.' Whenever she feared monsters, she gave a short spray and they were gone. All of us got more sleep."

One of the best responses I've heard to the classic, "How come he gets to do it when I couldn't at his age?" wail comes from the director of a child development center: "Because we learned that our approach wasn't successful in teaching the lesson so we're trying something different." It's explanatory, positive, and non-threatening to the child who asks. It also puts an end to the discussion.

Story-telling is an inexpensive and overlooked device for getting through tough times. Kids love parent stories, even if

they don't make sense. Hair-washing in our family was a trau-
matic event. Our young kids resisted being shampooed in the
tub or shower.

Frazzled, I began stretching them across the kitchen
counter and hanging their head over the sink to shampoo
them. The secret of the operation was my stories. If they didn't
fuss, I would tell a story based on the characters of children I
created: Boo Boo and Nicky. If they began to fuss, I stopped the
telling. I deliberately heightened the suspense whenever my
little captive began to squirm.

The other two kids and any odd friends would also stand
close, listening. I put Boo Boo and Nicky in cliff-hanging situations at the end of each child's shampoo so the next would be
eager to be shampooed so the story could go on. One time, they
even asked a neighborhood child to be shampooed so I would
extend the story.

The same technique worked on long auto trips. When the
kids got restless, I would begin reading or telling a story and
would continue as long as they behaved well. If anyone started
whining or bickering, I simply stopped and the others would
pressure the offender into behaving quietly.

An article featuring how chefs cook at home and how their
children react to their dishes brought a smile to my face. One
chef couple, the Schmidts, have a rule that the kids must at least
try everything once. Two comments from their tactful kids,
"That tastes pretty good; maybe I'll like it when I grow up," and
"I'm going to save my salad until later when I get big."

Many families struggle with getting a good family photo
for Christmas or other occasions. Often, the children refuse to
cooperate. Oh, how I wish we had the following idea when we
were taking our annual holiday photo. A dad told me they
bribed their children into posing pleasantly by promising them
that if they did, he would take a monster photo at the end of
the session. On this "take," they could make any face and

assume any monstrous position they liked. His children are grown now. "Those photos have become their most treasured ones," he said.

A woman named Susan wrote, "I couldn't resist writing you about what I think was my most brilliant comeback to, 'None of my friends have to do this much work. They get to have more fun. It isn't fair.'

"One of my four daughters said this to me and this wonderful answer popped into my head. 'Jill, when you grow up and get married and have children of your own, I want you to be sure and let them have all the fun. Don't make them do the dishes or fold the laundry, empty the trash or pick up their rooms. You do it. That way your kids will get to have all the fun, and you'll get to do all the work!'

"She went a little red in the face, but quickly began putting the laundry away, and I haven't heard that particular statement since."

Here's another creative response from a mother. "It might have been my birthday or perhaps an anniversary when first I tried a new technique for handling squabbles between our two school-aged girls. Paula came storming into the kitchen complaining loudly about her sister, Laura. I stopped her with, 'Paula, I am having a very nice day. Please don't spoil it with your fighting. Why don't you write down whatever you want to tell me and I promise you I will read it later—before I go to bed tonight, for sure?' I told her sister to do the same.

"They marched off, scribbled their complaints furiously and returned, satisfied for the moment, back to their play. This worked beautifully. It was easy to discuss their differences the next day when the heat of the fight had passed. Sometimes the solutions were obvious, as when Paula wrote, 'Laura won't stop yelling at me and telling lies no matter how much I yell at her.'

"One of my favorites was when Laura wrote, 'Don't believe anything Paula wrote.' She admitted later with a giggle that she could not remember what they were fighting about and had to come up with this imaginative defense.

"One day when a disgruntled Paula came in with a complaint and I answered calmly, 'Write it down,' she said, 'It's not worth the trouble.'

"'Then it's not worth troubling me about, either,' I said. Very little writing was done that day.

"Paula will be married later this month, and Laura will be her bridesmaid. They laugh when they remember writing their complaints and accusations, and they wish I had saved them so they could read and enjoy them today."

A common frustration of parents occurs when another child jumps into the argument going on between parent and child. We solved this by turning to the interloper and asking, "Do you want in on this? Because if you do, the outcome will be the same for you as for her." This ended the practice of choosing up sides during an argument in our family.

A mother shared, "My mother was constantly asked, 'What's for dinner?' by my four brothers and dad coming in from farm work. Her standard answer came to be, 'Shutupandeat.' Eventually, my brothers started coming in and asking, 'Are we having some more of that Shudupandeat?' She didn't have to waste her breath anymore. Just nodded."

Parents who are toilet training boys might appreciate hearing about my husband's trick in helping our sons learn to hit their target. He wadded up a few "boats" of toilet tissue, tossed them in, and said, "Let's sink 'em."

This insight comes from a mother of four children, ages seven, nine, seventeen, and nineteen. "Because we have about ten years between sets of children, we have a statement that we use occasionally that is said in jest, but also truthful to a degree: 'The only difference between a six and sixteen-year-old is ten years.' Many of the challenges facing a six-year-old—getting wheels (a bike), being more independent, going on her own to friends' homes farther away from our home—are the same challenges facing a sixteen-year-old—getting wheels, wanting more independence, going ever farther away.

"Their emotional state is very similar, too, especially from two to four and from twelve to fourteen. At least, that is some of the behavior we've observed. Of course, it is dealt with on a different level for each age group.

"An example is when children complain about being bored at age five or so. The best answer is, 'That's okay.' Children shouldn't be entertained and busy every moment. They need to know what boredom is and that it's okay to feel that way because it will happen to them ten years later. They need to learn early how to get themselves out of boredom in an appropriate and constructive way so they don't turn to drugs or other destructive activities simply to keep from being bored."

"When my kids got old enough to cook," a mom shared, "I posted a note on the door stating, 'The first one who asks what's for dinner will be the designated meal-planner and food-fixer tonight.' Everyone raced to their rooms and prayed someone else would ask first.

"Also, when my children want me to settle an argument they're having, they must sign a paper agreeing to abide by my decision with no complaints before I'll even agree to listen to the problem. Generally they prefer to solve it themselves."

Sometimes parents can get hooked into anger by a child's pouting or muttering. We had a child adept at each so we developed several responses. We muttered simultaneously as we went about our work, ceasing when the mutterer did. Or we acknowledged his behavior with, "You get three minutes of mutter," or "Great pout. How long do you think you can hold it?" Most often, we all ended up laughing.

A mother wrote, "We served liver and onions once a month, and the kids hated it. When the eldest was leaving for college, our younger daughter said, 'When Mary is gone will I still have to eat liver?'

"Her father responded, 'Yes, and we're going to mail Mary's portion to her.'"

One of my favorites came from a mother who obviously knows how to lighten up.

"Every once in a while families have bad days where nothing seems to go right and everybody is squabbling. My favorite way of changing the mood is to serve dessert first and tell everyone that if they don't eat every bit of dessert, they won't get any dinner at all. Another time, for dessert I served plates of whipped cream with a cherry buried in the middle. No utensils were allowed and everyone was blindfolded and had to sit on their hands. Everyone put a dime on the table. Whoever finished cleaning their plate first won the money. It sure improved our family's mood."

When our kids continued to fight after a warning to move their squabble out of our hearing, we came up with an effective stopper. "You get the east end of the backyard and you get the west end. Holler all you want but no touching or crossing lines. When you get tired of fighting, you can play in the whole yard or back in the house." It worked, especially in winter.

A mother wrote, "You're having trouble getting along today. I want you to sit down and each list three more things you want to fight about today. Then we'll set the time and you *will* fight about one for five minutes. Then you can take a break and we'll have the next fight. But make it good because once those three are done, so are you."

Mindy shared her technique of twisting replies into such complicated arguments that her daughter complies in order to stop the barrage. "To, 'You are the meanest mother!' I replied, 'Omygosh Kelly, the meanest? Now let's see, I mean I know I'm pretty mean, but the meanest? Gosh, Cinderella's step-mother, now *she* was meaner, I think, and wow, think of Hansel and Gretel's mother, she got the kids lost in the forest *on purpose*. . . . that's *really* mean . . .' and I go on and on until she cries, 'Uncle.'

"When she asked, 'Mom, can I get my ears pierced?' I said, 'Of course, honey, when you are 75. Too old? 62? 53? Okay, okay, 49. Still too long? 37? Hmmm, okay, tell you what. You can have them pierced when you are old enough to drive a car.' She's grateful I've been so flexible and willing to compromise."

Now *there's* a creative parent.

CHAPTER TEN

Tell Them We Love Them

Of the collective wisdom I've gathered from older parents over the past twenty years, the statement I treasure most came from a fifty-something grandmother who, after pondering my question on how she would change her parenting if given a second chance, said, "I'd tell them every day that I loved them."

When I pass that message on to groups of parents, most of the older parents nod in agreement. We wish we had focused less on criticism and more on love. We've learned that children pretty much turn out the way they're intended to turn out in spite of our best efforts to change their basic design. We realize that if we had affirmed them more for who they were and loved them more openly, they would have had an easier time learning to love themselves.

Parental anxieties over children's behavior are like rattles in the car. A few rattles indicate serious problems and need to be addressed to keep the car running smoothly, but most are minor annoyances on the trip. When we focus on the rattles, we miss the pleasures of the trip. Many parents focus so intently on children's behavior and achievement that they miss the scenery and joys of the parenting journey.

Regrettably, it is only in retrospect that we realize how many pleasures we have ignored along the way. It is in retrospect that we learn that the child who grew up with the messiest room keeps a tidy apartment when living alone, or we watch the child who was lackadaisical over homework turn into an overachieving adult. It is in retrospect that we admit to the limitations of our power in nurturing a child into adulthood.

We wish we had understood earlier that each child is his or her own person, one who is in training to become an adult. We are coaches, not creators. And, like good coaches, we know that caring, encouragement and acceptance are more effective than pressure, criticism, and conditional love in turning out either a fine athlete or healthy adult.

Ironically, many of the rattles of childhood become cherished memories in later life. I have a son who talks back to television, especially the commercials. When he was a teen living at home, his habit annoyed me but when he visits as a young adult and harangues the set, I enjoy it. I realize how much I miss it. I tell him so, and we laugh together. This same son has an infectious giggle which has always lightened the family mood. Whether he was delighting in cartoons as a child or in *Saturday Night Live* as a teen, we could hear his giggle throughout our home and it made us smile.

I don't know, however, that we ever told him *at the time* just how pleasurable his giggle was to us. And that's the pity. That's what the grandmother was saying when she said she'd tell her children every day that she loved them. We don't hesitate to point out weaknesses and misdeeds to our children, but we often neglect to affirm behaviors that give us joy.

There are many ways of telling children we love them. We don't have to stare into their eyes and say, "I love you." Just a casual comment or gesture meets the daily minimum requirement of appreciation and love that all of us treasure. If we take that grandmother's advice, we'll make a point of finding some way every day to show our children that they are loved.

And I don't mean by cooking their favorite foods. "Look at all I do for them; they should know I love them," is a common parent rationalization. But everyday parental services are not enough. Children don't equate service with love until they have children of their own. In their tender growing-up years, they yearn to be affirmed verbally and nonverbally by those they love most—parents.

Here are some easy ways to tell our children daily that we love them.

I missed you.
It's so good to have you back.
I love your laugh.
You make me feel good.
I'm glad you're ours.
Thanks for being you.
Come sit next to me for a minute.
You're my favorite first-born (middle-born, last-born,
    ten-year-old, etc.)
You're special.
Fantastic!
Awesome!
Life is nicer when you're around.
Maybe you don't need a hug, but I do.
I wouldn't trade you for any kid.
How did you get so lovable?
We lucked out getting a kid like you.
I knew you could do it.
You made my day.
Your smile makes me smile.
Where did you learn to do that so well?
What would we do without you?
I'm proud when people ask if I'm your dad.
Super job.
What I especially like about you is . . .
The world needs more kids like you.
Where have you been? I need a lift.
You make a difference around here.
I can't imagine life without you.
I love you more than chocolate.
Thanks for being you.

If parents find these uncomfortable to say because they didn't hear them as children themselves, they can use nonverbal expressions of love to get started:

a wink
a squeeze on the arm, shoulder, hand
"high five"
thumbs up
back or foot rub
shoulder massage
a tickle while passing
a loving look
shoulder lock
shared secret smiles, grins, laughter

We older parents don't want to live in retrospect, but we are saddened when we witness young parents making the mistakes we did. We wish they could overlook behaviors that are not worth the hassles and that they would become a communicating rather than arguing family. We've learned that formerly worrisome issues and conflicts disappear in the mist of memory while love endures beyond messy rooms, loud music, and sibling rivalry. We pass our experiences and wisdom on to young parents with a heartfelt message: "Lighten up and enjoy the trip."

Handy Responses to Kids' Argument Starters

Here's a reference list of children's classic questions or comments that raise parent hackles as well as a variety of responses designed to lower them. Many of them I have mentioned earlier in the book, but I offer these as a handy compilation for parents who don't have time or patience to thumb through the text when they need a quick response.

I repeat my caution against misusing these responses. They are not meant to be used sarcastically or unkindly but in tones of empathy, concern, humor, enthusiasm, explanation, puzzlement, apology, and the like. If parents use them as sarcastic or belittling one-liners, conflict and lower child self-esteem are sure to result.

To give kids an equal opportunity, I am starting with parent questions and comments that most irritate children, in the hopes that parents interested in establishing a more hassle-free home might eliminate or limit their use of them. Over the years, I've asked kids to list the remarks they most hated to hear from parents and discovered remarkable agreement.

What Kids Hate to Hear From Parents

How many times do I have to tell you?
Because . . .
Do as I say, not as I do.
What's wrong with you?
When I was your age . . .
Think of the starving children in . . .
If you don't like it, tough.
I've told you a thousand times . . .
Because I said so.
Wipe that smile off your face.
I'll give you something to cry about.
What will the neighbors think?
I won't love you if . . .
Why can't you be more like . . . ?
You'll put your eye out.
Do you want us to end up in the poorhouse?
You're eating us out of house and home.
I'm washing my hands of you.
I'm doing this for your own good.
It takes one to know one.
I've only got two hands.
This hurts me more than it does you.
Wait till your father gets home.
If it's worth doing, it's worth doing well.
Money isn't everything.
If everyone else jumped off a cliff, would you jump off too?
Someday I hope you have a child just like yourself.
Only a mother could love you.
Why don't you grow up?
Where did you lose it?
As long as you're living under this roof . . .
Who was that on the phone?
How was your day?
I love you, but . . .
Who's going to be at the party?
Get a job.
If you can't say anything nice, don't say anything at all.
Be careful.
Turn down that music!

Parental Responses to Kids' Classic Protests

Nonverbal Responses:

Sad sigh followed by a dreamy gaze into the distance
Non-stop expression of puzzlement
Expression of surprise or delight
Expression of intense sadness, head down
Pursed lips and concentrated thought
Incredulous stare into eyes of child
Wink
Loving smile
Indulgent smile
Full face grin
Surprise hug
Write something on a note while scrutinizing child.
Concentrate on twirling a yo-yo.
Remove file from jeans pocket and begin manicure.
Glance at watch and jot down time.
Adopt position of The Thinker.
Close eyes and inwardly recite Pledge of Allegiance or Lord's
Prayer or both.
Saunter away.

Verbal Responses to Nonverbal Behaviors Like Pouting, Eye-Rolling, Smirking, the Stone Face:

(Smile) *I love it when you look like that.*
How can you keep your face like that for so long?
Don't your lips get tired?

Great pout. Do you think you can hold it till Dad gets home?
What do you see up there?
Is there something in your eye?

You seem to have difficulty focusing today. Maybe we should see
   an optometrist.
When you do that, it reminds me of my uncle who
   (recite long story*).*
You've got a good face for pouting. Lots of people don't.

(With solicitude) *Does it hurt to keep your lip (or face) like that?*
I've never been able to pout. Will you teach me?
I'm glad you pout instead of complain. It's easier on my ears.

Time-Out Responses:
I'm not sure what to do right now.
I need some time to think about you.
Why not go to your room and think about it?

When you talk like that, I can't listen.
I feel a mad coming on, so I'm leaving for a few minutes.
I (or you) need some time alone to sort this out.

Ask me tomorrow after I've thought about it tonight.
You may be right. Then again, I may be right.
Let's give it some time.
Hmmm. That's an interesting argument.

You hurt my feelings when you talk like that. So I don't feel like
   listening right now.
We both know now how the other feels. So what do you think we
   should do about it?
You're enjoying yourself more than we are so why don't you go to
   your room and enjoy yourself by yourself?

When Kids Fight

You get three minutes of fight. After that, I'll separate you with some chores I've been saving.

If you can't play together, you can't play together.

It's your fight, and you have a right to it. I don't want to play.

I'm separating you for an hour. Maybe you'll get along better then because you'll be older.

Hmmm . . . this is the same fight as yesterday's. You must like it. Don't let me interrupt.

I know you like to fight, but I don't like to hear it. Please take it to where I can't hear it.

I need a time out. I'm going to my room until it's more peaceful around here **or** You need a time out. Go to your rooms until you decide to be peaceful.

Yes, you each have a point. Go to your room and write it down and bring it to me.

Oh, good. I was hoping for some fight-help. One of you sweep the patio, please, and the other straighten all the towels in all the bathrooms.

Uh oh, I see television violence is rubbing off on you. We'll give you a rest from it today and see if you're more peaceful tomorrow.

You better take a two minute sit-down here and watch the others play. Maybe you can learn from them.

When you can agree on what to watch, you can turn it back on.

How to Avoid Playing "First Sergeant"

It's time to get ready (as opposed to, "Get ready").

When you finish that chapter, please set the table.

After your phone call, rake the leaves, please.

Is there any reason why you can't empty the garbage before dinner?

When all our rooms are cleaned, we'll turn on TV.

Would you rather do the dishes now, or after your bath?

Responses to Persistent Tattlers

*I'm glad **you** didn't do it.*
Please go write your tattle down for me so I don't forget it.
There's a tattle list on the refridge. Will you put a check by your name, please?

You're the best tattler we have. How did you get so good?
Thank you for telling me. (When child responds, *"Aren't you going to do anything about it?"*) *Thank you for telling me.* Repeat, repeat, repeat.
Are you telling me because you care for John or because you're trying to get him into trouble?

Is this something I need to know or something you just want to tell?
I like you as much as I like him. Tattling doesn't make me like you more.
Let's see, you get three tattles a day. How many is this?

Sometimes tattling is easier than learning to get along, isn't it?
Now that you've tattled, why not try getting along? Do you think you're old enough for that?

Responses to "It's not fair."

True.
A lot of things aren't.
I know. It's the pits, isn't it?

You're probably right. Now, go do it.
Put up with me. I've never figured out how to be fair all the time.
Isn't that the truth? I was just thinking about that when you were arguing.

Fair is only a place where you go on rides and eat cotton candy.
There's a county fair and a state fair, but I've never heard of a "life fair."
So, who said it would be fair?

It's not a circus, either.
Yes, sometimes things in life aren't fair.

Responses to "How come I have to . . . ?"

Because I like you best.
Being strong and gorgeous has its price.
You were lucky enough to be here.

I said, 'God, send me some good help!' and look who God sent.
I cared enough to ask the very best.
I missed you, and your cheery face gives me a lift.

I didn't have time to go through the Yellow Pages for help.
Because I love to torture my children.
Because I feel like picking on you today.

Because it builds character.
Because it's got to be done.
Because your mother is a mean witch.

Consider it your contribution to the family.
I'm a witch, but I'm a modern witch. I ride a vacuum cleaner
   instead of a broom.
Sometimes you just luck out.

Because it will make you a better person.
Because I'm your mom. God gave me that job like I'm giving you
   this one.

Responses to "In a minute . . ."

Okay, sixty seconds it is.
Make it sooner.
Okay, I'm setting the timer. I'll expect you when it goes off.

Of what year?
The Time is Now!
10, 9, 8, 7,6, 5, 4, 3, 2, 1, 1/2, 1/4 . . . minute's up.

If the whole world ends in the next minute and Jesus comes for the
   second time, I don't want this house to be a mess.
I'll be generous and give you five. Then it's Mom Blastoff Time.

Responses to "He looked at me."

Congratulations. You've got his attention.
I don't blame him. I like to look at you, too.
Being gorgeous carries a price.

Look right back at him.
It's 'cause you're so handsome.
We stare at people we love, don't we, Eric?

How interesting. I'm looking at you, too.
Well, you just look right back at him. It will serve him right.
How did you know? Were you looking at him?

Do something gross, and he'll stop.
Well, he didn't hit you or spit on you, so smile back at him. It will
    drive him nuts.

Responses to "All the other mothers . . . /none of the other dads . . ."

Name three. Write them down. And don't forget their phone
    numbers.
Let me introduce myself. My name is Mrs. Your Mother.
They don't feed you, do they? In fact they don't even know you,
    do they?

But you don't live with them.
Be sure you get the right address if you plan on living there.
Would you like to trade me in on a new mom?

I know. I'm sorry, Honey. It's the luck of the draw.
All the other parents are nicer than we are.
All the other kids agree with their parents.
All the other kids think I'm wonderful, too.

Responses to "I did it the last time."
And so well.
You ate last time, too.
You were the last? You'll be the first this time.

Good. Then you know how.
I did it the two times before that.
Was it for the last time? Does the same hold for driving you to soccer?

Do it this time, too.
No, last time I did it, but I didn't bother you by asking.
It would be a shame to waste all that practice.

See if you can make a trade. Otherwise, it's yours.
That's life in the big kitchen.
I know. I always think maybe it's the last time I have to do your laundry, but it hasn't happened yet.

Will you write down that you're doing it this time and put a date on it so I'll remember next time?
Isn't it boring to have to keep doing the same things—like mowing the lawn and cooking dinner?

Responses to "Last time you let me . . ."
***This** is the last time.*
Give me credit for learning.
You ate last time, too. Make the connection.

That was then, and this is now.
This time I'm not letting you.
I had a lapse of consciousness.

Keep pushing and it may be the last time I let you.
I must have been brain-dead that day.
It's a wise parent who is flexible.

Responses to "Whenever . . ."/"Whatever . . ."

Is that longer or shorter than "Just a minute"?
Whenever just started.
Whenever is an adverb, not an o'clock.

Really? Whatever I want? Wow!
What ever inspired you to give such a thoughtful response?
That's a wonderfully concise reply but it lacks a little in brilliance.

Better ponder it for awhile and come up with a better answer
before dinner, phone, or TV.

You must be too tired to think. I get that way at times. We'd like
you to go to bed an hour earlier tonight to help you think
better tomorrow.

Responses to "I hate you."

(Sigh) *And I love you so much.*
All I ask is that you respect me. You can love me later.
I suppose you do. That's okay for now.

That's part of life. Look at all the wars.
I'm sorry you feel that way but it doesn't change things.
    I still love you.
Oh, dear, you'll have to stand in line.

That's how you feel right now. Maybe you won't next week.
Then I must be doing something difficult, but right.
You hate me, and I love you. Guess that's my problem.

Responses to "Because . . ."

'Because' is a preposition and it requires an object. What's your
    object?
'Because' is a conjunction, not an answer.
Embellish, please.

Wow. Your education is paying off.
That's cute. I remember when you were three and you answered
    everything with "cuz."

Responses to "Why are you looking at me like that?"

I can't help it . . . you're so gorgeous.
My eyes wander at times.
I like what I see most of the time.

I love that expression on you.
Because I love you.
People always look at those they love.

I'm just wondering how we were so lucky to get you.
To see if you still look like you did yesterday.
Because your expression is so interesting and unusual.
Because I like the way your face scrunches up when you're thinking.

Responses to "Just because he's youngest/ oldest/bigger/little . . ."

Funny. Your sister just said that about you.
You're right. Ageism, sexism, and sizeism are against the law in this house.
God made that decision, not I. Complain to him.

That's not my reason, it's yours.
No, I just like him better at the moment.
You're right. What a drag.

Responses to "It's not my fault."

But it's your burden.
I understand how you feel. It's hard facing the consequences of our actions.
It's not mine, either.

You're great. It's your messiness that's a problem.
Must be the leprechaun who lives here.
Let's investigate the crime. You be the detective and bring me all the evidence. I'll be the judge.

Responses to "I didn't do it."
Good. What **did** you do?

Neither did I. Clean it up, please.

I'm so glad. I can't imagine anyone doing it. Clean it up, please.

Nobody did. Isn't that a mystery?

I know. I hate it when I have to clean up what I didn't do.

Casper the Ghost is on the loose again. Since nobody did it, everybody needs to be on the alert.

Gather everybody in the kitchen, and let's all find out who did. If we can't, we'll clean it up together.

I understand. But please explain what happened.

Responses to "I'm not going."/"I don't want to go."
Let me have all your reasons in writing within the next hour.

A fourteen-year-old will look awfully funny in a baby stroller.

This sounds like a power struggle. Do you know what a power struggle is? Well, it's where . . . (elaborate until child becomes bored; if he/she continues, start over.)

I don't want to go, either. Let's go and support each other.

Good, you can clean your closet and drawers and have dinner ready for us.

But we love your company, and we want so much to be the Brady Bunch.

Just humor me. I'm an old lady.

Neither do I. Let's talk about our reasons in the car.

I understand that, but I need your help.

I know. Isn't it awful to have to go places you don't want to?

Yes, family reunions (or church or whatever) can be boring so let's go and see if we can find a bright spot in this one.

I know how you feel. I don't like to go to pack meetings either.

Responses to "Why are you so mad?"

I don't know why. (Sigh). *I guess I'm picking it up from you kids.*
I'm mad because I know how lovable you really can be.
Because I love you too much to give up on you.

It feels good to get mad when others don't treat you right, doesn't it?
I bet you thought only kids could get mad.
Mad is catching. When I hear you arguing, I catch it from you.

MAD stands for Mom Ain't Delighted (or any of following list)*:*
   Defeated, Deaf, Dumb, Delaying, Deluded, Dense,
   Disappearing, Distracted, Disrespected, Docile, Daft,
   Doing it, Done. (Memorize list and choose the one that
   best fits. Or use them all for emphasis. Then add, *"Do*
   you want to know why?")

Responses to "What's for dinner?"

I don't know.
Good stuff.
I don't want to spoil it for you.

Ground warm sandwiches on toast.
I'm not sure. Something that thawed accidentally.
Oh, I knew there was something I was supposed to do.

Two choices: take it or leave it.
Stone soup.
Green eggs and ham.

Ask your father.
Mud pie, frog eyes . . . the usual.
Something you'll like.

Zukahavi with ricochet.
Bees' knees and mosquito knuckles.
Spinach, liver, and onions. (Same answer daily)

Oh, ick. I don't even want to think about it.
Whatever you plan on making.
Ohhhh, I don't know. I'll think about it tomorrow.

Doof. (It takes a while to figure this one out.)
Check the blackboard. It has today's special on it.
Consternation stew.

A delicious healthy well-balanced color-coordinated masterpiece.
A recapitulation of last night's fabulous feast.
Same thing as last Wednesday.

Chef's surprise. ("What's that?") That's the surprise.
*Something that has 3 grams of fat, 4 of carbohydrates, lots of fiber
    and 410 calories.*
You get three guesses, and if you're right, you get served first.

*Parsnips and grits. ("Yuck.") I knew you'd say that so you'll be
    happy when you find out what we're really having.*
*I'm glad you're interested. It's an old Midwest recipe which has its
    origins in* (go on and on until they wish they hadn't asked).
I really don't know, but it was on sale.

My own new recipe. After we eat it, we'll name it.
Al fresco alfredo florentine. ("What's that?") What's in front of you.
Smorgasbord
Salad, meat, and potatoes . . . I think.

Responses to "It's yucky."/"What is it?"/"I don't like it."

First one to figure it out wins dessert.

That's okay, honey. My feelings aren't hurt if you don't like it.

I know you don't, but breakfast always tastes so good when you don't eat the night before.

Neither do I very much. I hate cooking something I don't like.

When I don't like something, I eat it first to get it over with.

Neither does your cousin Mary. I remember the time. . . . (long story)

If we eat it all tonight, I promise we won't have it tomorrow.

I'm glad to know that. I'll keep it in mind when I'm tempted to cook it again.

If it tasted good, it probably wouldn't be good for you.

I don't know, but it's brown and lumpy. What do you think we should call it?

Nobody has to eat anything. It will hold till tomorrow night.

The next person who complains about the food makes dinner tomorrow.

Talk about yuck! How would you like to have to cook this?

Is it on your list of three free yucky foods? No? Too bad. Oh, well, you can put it on next month's list.

But, oh, so nourishing.

You're probably right.

Boy, are we lucky to get one who won't eat us out of house and home.

So is roof tar (to "It's yucky").

But it will put hair on your chest.

No, it's not. I didn't use any of my Yucky spice—just salt and pepper.

Responses to "I didn't get to do it at her age."

Neither did I.
I can't remember that far back.
We probably should have let you.
I know. When we saw what worked and what didn't, we changed things.

We were younger then.
You were doing other things at her age.
Let me tell you the parable of the vineyard—about the workers who complained about the latecomers who got paid the same . . .
(you only have to tell it once).

And look how you turned out.
What a memory you have! What did we have for dinner the time we didn't let you do it at her age?

You were the forerunner, the stalking horse. You cleared the obstacles for her. Isn't she lucky to have you sacrifice so much?
How old were you at her age?
Is that right? How time flies.

She's lucky she's younger than you, isn't she? Should we let her be older than you for awhile and see how it feels?
I guess she's just older than you were at her age.
Your memory is short.

The speed of time has increased the past five years.
We were experimenting then. We know more now.
Are you afraid that we liked her more at that age?

Responses to "I don't have any homework."

That's good, but the homework hour still holds. Find a good book.
Then how about some housework?
That's great. This is a good evening to brush up on your spelling.

I'll give you a list.
Wonderful. Write a two-page letter to Grandma and bring it to me
  for spelling before you recopy it.
Show me the homework you don't have.

Good. I have a few jobs around here.
Then we can go over some of your math tables (or learn the state
  capitals or write a story about fishing).
This will give you a chance to read, then. If you can't find a
  book, I'll find one.

I was hoping someone didn't. I need some recipes recopied, and it
  will give you a chance to practice your handwriting.
Good. Let's go for a family drive.
Write that down, date it, sign it, and I'll save it for the next parent
  conference.
*Great. Here's **my** assignment.*

Responses to "But dad said . . ."

Dad and I work together. We're partners.
Dad is usually right. I'd better find out what he meant.
Dad said he trusted me to give you the right answer.

Dad told me he loves you too much to let you risk danger.
Did Dad say he wanted you to talk like this?

Responses to "You don't trust me."

I trust you. It's the situation I don't trust.
No, but I love you.
Trust isn't at issue here. Beer parties are.

(Sigh) I guess I just love you too much. That's a problem I have.
This isn't a matter of trust. We can argue that another time. Let's
  deal with the issue of curfew.
And you don't trust me if you think I'm doing this for me.

Responses to "Get a life, Mom."/"Get real, Dad."

This is as real as I get.

Didn't we ever tell you? We got you life.

This is all the life I want, especially at the moment.

Which life, yours or mine?

I tried it once, but it was too expensive.

(Poetically) *Life is a bowl of cherries, a rainbow of colors, an assortment of people and a glorious opportunity to love.*

Fantasy is more fun.

Responses to "You always . . ."/"You never . . ."

Yes, I'm afraid I'm the reliable sort.

You like "You always . . ." don't you?

Did you know that "always" is one of the most misspelled words in the English language?

And you always remind me of that. Thank you.

Always means all ways. Do me a favor and write down all the ways I do it.

Well, I never!

I'm glad you notice when I'm consistent.

I rarely understand "never." It's so final.

When you say that, I think I have to keep doing it. Otherwise I'd break my record.

Responses to General Complaints

Start complaining because I'm getting ready to tell you what we're going to do.

Yes, it's the pits. So let's start digging.

I'm impressed that you can change your voice like that.

I'm glad you complain so much. Then the rest of us don't have to.

You get three minutes of uninterrupted complaining. So get it all in because then you're through.

(With admiration) *Where did you learn to complain so well?*

Would you like to know how other kids handle this?

All-Purpose Responses
All-purpose classic: (smile lovingly and without any tinge of malice) *Someday, you may be lucky enough to have a child just as lovable as you.*
Oh, really?
Thank you for sharing.

If you have to ask that question, you'll never understand the answer.
Why do you ask? **or** *What makes you think that?* **or** *What would make you say that?*
No, it's **our** *room and we're letting you use it till you're out on your own.*

Let's pray about it.
(Sigh). *The burdens of responsibility lie heavily on a parent's shoulders.*
I'm hurt. I depended on you and the job wasn't done. (Kids should feel guilty when they're guilty.)

Thank you. Parenting is a learning process, and your input helps.
It's okay to hate doing it but you have a choice: you can do it with consequences or without. You **will** *do it.*
What part of "No" don't you understand? I'll be happy to explain it again.

Do you all agree that life is more pleasant around here when I'm happy?
Are you saying you're not sure it can be done or you can't do it?
One divides the candy and the rest choose.

I need a reason why you can't (clean up your mess, finish your homework, etc.)?
Dinner's not late. It's not ready.
I learned that at Mean Mom School.

I have faith in you.
How would you solve this if you were me and I were you?
I guess I just love you too much.

Because God sent me to you and you to me. Who knows the will of God?
I hope you'll do better when you're a dad with a kid like you.
Is this worth the fight? Let's examine that first.
We'll discuss it when you're a little older—like maybe tomorrow.

Responses to Miscellaneous Remarks

I'm running away:
Okay, but take your clothes off before you go. You came to us
   naked—you'll leave us naked.
Okay, but you can't cross any streets.
Hey, I'm Mom, and I get to run away first. Then you can.

I'm not perfect:
Yes, dear, I know.

I'm bored:
That's okay.

I didn't ask to be born.
I'm sad you're in pain.

I don't have my homework (uniform, project etc.)
How are you going to solve your problem? I'm not as concerned
   about the problem as much as I am in how you can solve it.

If I tell you, do you promise not to get mad?
No, but I promise to forgive you. (Tantrum) That must make you
   tired. Want a rest?

You don't understand me.
No, but I don't let that get in the way of love.

Dolores Curran

lectures and writes widely on parenting and family life. The author of fourteen books, including the best-seller *Traits of a Healthy Family*, her articles have appeared in *Reader's Digest*, *McCall's*, *Redbook*, and *Parents Magazine*. The mother of three young adults, she lives with her husband Jim in Littleton, CO.